To

John, Fliss

and Greg

who have weathered

every word of it

Contents

1 Writing as a means of inquiry

Places of learning and inquiry; the three "cultures": humanities, sciences and social sciences; differences in substance, methodology and argumentation between disciplines

2 Essay questions

The instruction: checking the instruction word, its value among surrounding words; the key terms, non-technical, technical and theory-laden; value words and the criteria underlying them; a central proposition and how to work one out

3 Writing to inform

Organizing information by means of (a) natural schemes, that is, ones based on time, process, or cause and effect; or (b) artificial schemes, that is, ones based on generality, importance, comparison, or problem and solution; explaining how and why

4 Writing to influence

Interpretive essays   Evaluative essays
Argumentative essays   **39**

Interpreting: looking for trends in your data or themes to empha-size, and expressing a theme through a key phrase or model; responding to a ready-made interpretation; evaluating: setting up your criteria; pre-professional evaluations; arguing: finding the grounds for argument in your data, or in common assumptions, or both; argumentative strategies: to aim for impact or conciliation

5 Information at a glance

Introductions and conclusions   Tables and graphs
Diagrams, drawings and maps   **54**

Essay introductions: to stimulate interest and mould the reader's expectations; essay conclusions, relevant to type of discussion; non-verbal summaries of information: use of tables, graphs and diagrams to display and compare quantities; use of drawings and maps

6 Reports

The standard format   **69**

Introduction: the aim alone, or a discussion of the background liter-ature plus the research hypothesis; method, including materials, apparatus, procedures, subjects; results; discussion/conclusion for shorter and longer reports; abstracts and their components

7 Words and working with them   83

Words to express ideas (referential): the specialized *v.* colloquial, the abstract *v.* specific, denotations and connotations; words to bind the text together (textual): synonyms, antonyms and all-purpose words, conjunctives and the logical relationships they express; words to engage your reader (interpersonal): direct appeal, emphatic and absolute words, "hedge" words, negative elements, cues to the text's structure

8 Sentences and making a point   100

Individual sentences: shorter and longer, simple, compound and complex; managing the focus: topic and comment, topicalizing tech-niques incl. special phrases and the passive verb, topical progres-sions to move the discussion along; paragraphs and the index sentence

LIST OF FIGURES

LIST OF TABLES

To the student

If you have got as far as tertiary study, you are unlikely to be seeking help with the most basic aspects of writing. More likely you are concerned to make your writing really *work* for you, to deliver information competently, and to sustain a line of argument through a body of details.

Effective writing depends in the first place on having a clear sense of purpose. So the earlier chapters of this book are designed to show you ways of thinking about your writing task that will help you to define your purpose. The demands of writing vary somewhat from one discipline to another because of differences in their materials and methods (see chapter 1), and also because writing has more than one function in tertiary training. In the sciences, pure and applied, writing typically serves as a means of communicating established information (see chapter 3), while in the humanities it is much more often a means of exploring individual ideas and arguments (see chapter 4). Writing of both kinds is called for in the wide range of social science subjects. Any writing task thus reflects the character of the discipline in which it is set, although its purpose and scope are most closely defined by the terms of the question and by the proposition you choose to respond with. These things are discussed in chapter 2.

Any longer piece of writing also depends for its effectiveness on having a recognizable form, or structure. It may be conventional, as with reports, whose sections (introduction, method, etc.) supply the standard format for experimental writing in the sciences (see chapter 6). But for essays and tutorial papers there is no standard structure. You have to design your own, and ideally it is one that represents the shape of your material and the character of your message. It is a matter of breaking that material or message up into its component units and identifying the relationship between them. Having done that, you will be able to decide what is the best order or arrangement for those units, one which then underscores the organizing principle of the discussion. A number of possible structures are illustrated in connection with sample topics in chapters 3 and 4. It is assumed that you will also want to try out topics of your own against the suggestions made in those chapters. (There are additional assignment topics from many disciplines in appendix B.)

Whatever structure you choose for your essay or paper, it will be framed by an introduction and a conclusion, written to anticipate the reader's needs at either end of the discussion. Depending on the discipline, you may also want to include tables and other visual aids for the reader. All these are discussed in chapter 5.

Finally, effective writing depends on strategically chosen expression. Chapter 7 shows how the right word choices can help to engage readers' sympathies and sustain their interest in your writing, as well as serving to pinpoint information and ideas. The uses of different types of sentences are discussed in chapter 8, to show how they divide information into digestible pieces and how they control the ongoing focus of attention. Punctuation, a vital aid in indicating sentence structure, is discussed in chapter 9. (The various conventions on referencing and footnotes are also discussed in chapter 9.)

The strategies offered by this book are, of course, *thinking* strategies. They are ways of looking at your task and your material that will help you to handle them appropriately and effectively. The more time you give to thinking about the underlying purpose and structure of your writing, the more confidently you will write. And with the overall design worked out, you will be free to think more about details of expression and to exploit the resources of language for maximum communication with the reader.

1

Writing as a means of inquiry

Why write?

PLACES OF LEARNING AND INQUIRY

Present-day colleges, universities and institutes of higher education are indeed extraordinary places, when you think of the enormous range of subjects that are tackled there. In what other institution do people investigate matters as varied as:

- theories of sleep
- the microclimatic effects of windbreaks
- numerical operations that lead to a loss of accuracy
- paralinguistic forms of communication on radio
- the internal logic of *Das Kapital* . . .

to take only the merest sampling of topics from the exam papers of one Australian tertiary institution? Staff and students work together through thousands of topics like these each year, sifting through established facts and exploring new questions on all the frontiers of knowledge.

There was no such spread of subjects in the earliest colleges and universities. Both have evolved from smaller, more specialized institutions that concentrated on professional training in just one area, or at most two or three. Italy's first universities (Salerno, founded during the ninth century, and Bologna, early twelfth century) were each devoted to a single discipline, respectively medicine and law. The universities of Oxford and Cambridge were both founded in the thirteenth century to further the study of theology and law. These medieval universities were in fact corporations of specialists, and the word *university* at that time meant something like a professional union, a body set up to protect the interests of its members, to consolidate their expertise, and to train and recruit new members. The earliest colleges were also set up in association with a particular profession or craft, though not necessarily associated with teaching. The College of Cardinals, the (Royal) College of Surgeons, and the College of Heralds are ongoing institutions of this kind. But the members of such specialized institutions were of course well-equipped to train novices, and so teaching gradually became an important function of colleges too.

Teaching, training and educating are now the primary roles of colleges and universities, and they take responsibility for both the professional and the general education of students. Yet, while offering systematic training, they have always been centres of intellectual inquiry and debate. The topics have changed over the centuries but are still comparable. Questions of free will and predestination have given way to those concerning the public versus individual interest; and the medieval quest for a recipe for gold has been replaced by the quest to synthesize fuels inexpensively. The intellectual questions of the day have sometimes made educational institutions a battleground for rival forces and conflicting attitudes. Religious controversies that racked institutions of the sixteenth century have their twentieth-century counterparts in political issues that have been fought out on campuses in Europe, North America, Southeast Asia and Australia. At such times the pen has not always seemed mightier than the sword.

Colleges and universities are nevertheless committed to systematic study and reasoned inquiry; and the written word is, as it has always been, a central means of teaching and learning, of communicating what is known as well as exploring new possibilities. Both students and teachers use writing to record and relay knowledge and to establish coherent patterns of thought. We use it when exercising ourselves on the specific problems of a discipline and re-evaluating older theories in response to fresh discoveries. It provides expression for newly conceived ideas and registers them in a form in which we and others can critically assess them. Whether we are novices or veterans, writing is an instrument of learning and inquiry, a way of coming to terms with problems that challenge the disciplines we work in.

The academic problems and questions we write about are always posed in the context of a particular discipline, and this determines the nature of the question asked and the kind of answer expected. We may illustrate this with, say, questions about music, which might have to be discussed in acoustic, cultural or aesthetic terms, depending on whether they were set in a department of physics, anthropology, or music itself. The respective discussions would hardly seem to be "in the same language", and hardly even about "the same thing". In one, music would be treated as a set of acoustic patterns, in another as the product of a given culture, and in the third as aesthetic experience.

The music example helps to show how fundamental the differences between academic disciplines are. They are nevertheless, not so obvious when we move from a course in history to one in economics, or from one in anthropology to one in psychology, partly because the very differences in subject matter tend to mask other significant differences in methodology and argumentation. These differences tend to be taken for granted by the staff within each discipline, and are rarely talked about. But they are critical for students who have to take courses in more than one discipline, often before they've had time to get acquainted with any.

The differences begin with the characteristic subject matter of each discipline, but they extend from there to different methods of handling the data and particular ways of arguing a point of view. Each of these will be discussed in the next few pages.

THE THREE "CULTURES"

SUBSTANCE
Academic disciplines may be classed as belonging to one of three divisions: humanities, natural sciences, or social sciences.

These are sometimes referred to as "the three cultures", following C. P. Snow, the British scientist and novelist, whose contacts in both the scientific and literary world made him acutely aware of the differences between them. In a famous lecture in 1959 he spoke of a gulf in outlook and practice between those working in the humanities and those in the natural sciences, and called them "the two cultures"; but he later recognized the separate existence of the social sciences,[1] and hence the third "culture". The three cultures may be simply distinguished by their respective concern with the human, the natural and the social aspects of our world. The music example already given shows up these differences: music as a medium of special experience falls within the humanities, as a set of sound waves within the natural sciences, and as the product of culture within the social sciences.

As disciplines of study, the three are not equally old. Only the humanities can claim a continuous tradition back to the medieval university. Medieval medicine was not, of course, founded on modern scientific practices, and scientific method as we know it was pioneered during the seventeenth and eighteenth centuries by such men as Newton, Huygens and Lavoisier. The earliest chairs of chemistry, for instance, were set up in the eighteenth and nineteenth centuries. The pioneers of the social sciences, such as Frazer, Wundt and Durkheim, wrote in the nineteenth century, and tertiary studies in these areas developed only this century.

But what the newer sciences lack in tradition they more than make up in influence. The fields of scientific knowledge have expanded so dramatically through the application of scientific method that scholars in the humanities and social sciences have been challenged to apply similar methods in their own disciplines; hence such terms as **social science, linguistic science, historical science, political science**. And in the last few decades, methods developed in the social sciences, for instance in politics and anthropology, have been borrowed by some scholars in the humanities for the study of history and literature.

Before going into the methodologies of the disciplines, let us look more closely at the differences in the substances of the three cultures. The **humanities** have been expanding continuously over centuries,[2] from the study of just grammar, logic and rhetoric to a vast array of languages and literatures, histories and philosophies and arts. But all humanistic disciplines essentially engage us in the study of human experience, its nature and its various forms. Human experience may be vested in historical events and materials, in language (taken either for its own sake, or as a vehicle for literature and philosophy), or in other symbolic systems, such as art, film and music. The forms that embody human experience are very diverse, and scholars studying them may choose to highlight their individual qualities or their likeness to others in the same genre, which again contributes to the diversity of the humanities. But, broadly speaking, work in the humanities is geared to establishing common bases for responding to humanistic media and to setting appropriate values on them.

The **natural sciences** are concerned with the things of the natural world and with the chemical, physical, biological and geological processes that contribute to our environment. Work in these disciplines involves looking for patterns and regularities in natural phenomena and working out descriptions of them that will explain and predict the occurrences of other things. The natural sciences also form a foundation for the applied sciences, for example: engineering, medicine and agriculture, as well as the "building science" side of architecture. (This last clearly has a footing in the humanities too.)

The **social sciences** concern themselves with descriptions of the individual and society and relationships between them, again looking for patterns in individual and group behaviour. The collective behaviour of human beings can be viewed from many perspectives: anthropological, demographic, economic, legal, political, psychological, sociological, all of which yield separate disciplines for the study of society. Interest in social behaviour is also growing in some areas of the humanities, such as history, archaeology and linguistics (for language can be seen as a form of social interaction), and some courses in those disciplines have a good deal in common with the social sciences.

But as long as the historian's main interest is in sources, the archaeologist's in material evidence, and the linguist's in language, they still belong with the humanities. The essential difference between the social sciences and the humanities can be shown by the kinds of reference material each would use. For example, in discussing murder and the murderer's predicament, students in the social sciences would refer to a criminology textbook, and those in the humanities to something like Dostoevski's *Crime and Punishment*. (The autopsy would be source material for the natural sciences.)

METHODOLOGY

The methodology used in any discipline tends to be related to its subject matter, although we cannot divide academic methods neatly into three kinds corresponding to the human/natural/social divisions just described. In fact, the methods used in the disciplines of the humanities and social sciences are many and varied. In the **natural sciences**, however, the methodology is relatively uniform, hence its impact on non-scientific disciplines (an impact which some writers feel is unfortunate).[3] The natural sciences set themselves apart as a block for their use of empirical methods and inductive procedures. They stress the importance of detached and neutral observation of anything, and the need to test hypotheses and formulate theories on the basis of observed data. Their most common practice is the use of controlled experiments in which natural phenomena are quantified, permitting other scientists to check their findings. This is, of course, why students spend hundreds of hours in laboratories. The details and procedures of experiments are most often presented in the form of a report (see chapter 6), and its various sections are intended to show up the empirical nature of any investigation. Whether scientific activity is entirely empirical and objective is now questioned,[4] but empirical practices have a central place in the sciences, which they do not have in other disciplines.

The substance of the **social sciences** and humanities does not really lend itself to controlled experimentation. Researchers can hardly conduct economic or legal or political experiments, however dearly they would like to; and it is only in some areas of psychology, where aspects of human behaviour can be isolated for controlled observation, that the practices of the natural sciences are regularly used. Because such methods are not appropriate for the study of complex human behaviour, individual and social, researchers mostly work with data derived from ordinary social phenomena and sequences of events (that is, ones that are neither staged nor experimentally controlled). In discussions of the data there may be little attempt to present it free of theoretical interpretation, though this varies, theory being invoked much more promptly by, say, sociologists than anthropologists. But with social data it is difficult, perhaps impossible, to make observations in a strictly neutral way, independent of any prior theoretical or social assumptions. Reading and writing in the social sciences therefore call for a good deal of sensitivity to theoretical positions. It pays, for example, to watch out for references to the nature/nurture controversy in discussions of human behaviour and in explanations of behavioural data. They may link up with *unspoken* assumptions about the role of genes versus environment.

In the **humanities** all the methodologies described so far – and more – are to be found. The methods of the natural sciences are practised in some areas of linguistics (for example acoustic phonetics) where the raw material of speech (sound waves) can be handled by experimental procedures. The procedures of formal logic are used for some subjects in philosophy, as in pure mathematics. But most work done in the humanities is a matter of interpretation. It often means working with relevant theory to interpret the texts you have read (as in history or the older literatures). Interpretation may also be based on coordinated individual responses to the readings, an approach encouraged in the "practical criticism" schools of literature, and elsewhere. When writing in the humanities you need to know which of the possible modes of interpretation is preferred, and it may vary from course to course within the same discipline, depending on individual staff members. The reading lists (whether they contain secondary or just primary sources) will be a guide.

ARGUMENTATION

Successful academic writing involves the ability to argue points convincingly. A critical reader will be unmoved by bald assertions of a point of view and will wait to see what arguments are used to support it. Academic argumentation in fact proceeds mostly by the kind of informal logic that we use every day as we make assumptions about ordinary things. We usually make claims or assumptions on the basis of observation or some sort of fact, for instance:

George must have had a trying day — he is so grumpy.

In this case the observation "he is so grumpy" is the **grounds** for our **claim**. The grounds give explicit support to the claim. But the argument as a whole depends on an *implicit* piece of knowledge by which we recognize the relevance of the grounds to the claim: that people's behaviour late in the day often reflects what they have had to put up with earlier. This knowledge or understanding, not explicitly spelt out in the argument, is its **warrant**. (The term **warrant** may be new, but its usage should be familiar from the expression "unwarranted assumption".) Without an identifiable warrant there may be no clear relationship between the grounds and the claim, and the argument falls apart. This is the case with:

Honey goes well with porridge because it is 70 per cent invert sugar.

The claim and grounds are both there, and the grounds are a scientific fact, yet there is no satisfactory argument. The problem is that the grounds, however scientifically sound, are irrelevant to the gastronomic claim. Like certain kinds of advertising, the statement dazzles us with science but does not make an argument. The grounds do not relate to the claim, and there can be no common understanding of the relationship between the two to supply a warrant.

Academic arguments, like everyday ones, depend on having both grounds and claim, and a satisfactory warrant behind them. But the warrants used vary in their accessibility, and arguments in some disciplines may seem far from self-evident to those outside them. Consider the following arguments (the grounds have been italicized in each case):

1. The government of Iceland 1000 years ago was enlightened, *for it provided full democratic representation for every citizen.*
2. *Chaucer's ability to present a rich panorama of humanity* makes him our greatest medieval author.
3. *The reduction in the number of new city building projects* shows we are about to experience a recession.
4. *Because we live in the southern hemisphere,* we may expect water here to circulate clockwise down the plughole.

In the first two of these arguments we can immediately see how the grounds support the claim because both appeal to an understanding or general principle that we recognize and assume every reasonable person would share. In the others, especially the last, the relationship between grounds and claim is obscure unless we are acquainted with some specialized knowledge. There *is* a warrant to justify the argument, but it is not common knowledge.

In the humanities scholars work much of the time with arguments that depend on general warrants, that is, ones involving some common understanding or principle. Argument 1, that *the government of Iceland was enlightened* is warranted by the principle that all people have a right to participate in their own government, something that is generally agreed on and taken for granted today. There is no way of proving that people have such a right, but the principle has its strength in widely shared human values and is thus a satisfactory warrant.

Arguments that rely on warrants from common consensus and common human values are frequently used in the discussion of social, ethical and aesthetic issues. Argument 2, that *Chaucer is our greatest medieval author,* is another such case, and it takes for granted the principle that the primary function of literature is to portray human life. No doubt many readers would agree and accept the argument as fully warranted. On the other hand, the argument may seem less satisfactory to those who hold that there are other criteria of good literature, for instance, the technical merit of the work. Who is to say which is the ultimate criterion? Individual tastes often jostle with one another in aesthetic discussion, and the common values we may hope to appeal to are elusive.

Fortunately, there is still scope for aesthetic argumentation about literature. Even though the warrants for arguments like the one about Chaucer would not be accepted by every reader, they can still be used in conjunction with other arguments whose warrants are mutually compatible. Provided the arguments in a discussion are internally consistent, they can form a valid interpretation of a work, and one as valid as any other. The relativity of aesthetic arguments means, of course, that there is room for more than one approach and that no critic can have the last word on a piece of literature!

No common understanding or shared values supply the warrants for the other two arguments listed above. In each, the argument is validated by a specialized warrant, knowledge possessed by those trained in the field and not necessarily familiar to every man or woman in the street. In argument 3, that *the reduction in the number of new city building projects shows we are about to experience a recession*, the link between grounds and claim is supplied by a recognized economic phenomenon. It is the fact that the building industry is highly sensitive to a drop in general prosperity and is therefore a useful indicator of economic conditions. So the argument is neither speculative nor idiosyncratic, but has its warrant in specialized knowledge shared by economists and informed lay people.

Argument 4, *that we may expect water here (in Australia) to circulate clockwise down the plughole*, has its warrant in scientific knowledge, in the fact that objects or fluids moving towards a point on the surface of the rotating earth are deflected by the Coriolis force, and that they tend to circulate clockwise around the point in the southern hemisphere and anticlockwise in the northern (other things being equal). Without that specialized knowledge, it is far from evident how geography affects the direction in which water flows; but with it, the relationship between grounds and the claim is satisfactorily validated. In both arguments 3 and 4, the warrants are something we learn as part of training in the relevant discipline, unlike the warrants of arguments 1 and 2, which are accessible to non-specialists.

This is not to say that discussions in the humanities never use specialized warrants. In history or literature or philosophy, arguments may be raised that depend on specialized knowledge, just as in the examples taken from economics and physics. Yet the subject matter of the humanities gives much more scope for ethical and aesthetic arguments which, as we have seen, have their warrants in common values more or less widely shared. The same freedom to use non-specialized warrants is exercised in some disciplines in the social sciences, where particular arguments about society may turn on an appeal to certain ethical values. But in the professionally oriented disciplines in the social sciences, for example business administration and law, full use is made of arguments relying on specialized warrants, because decisions and judgments have to be justified or justifiable in terms of bodies of fact and precedent. Likewise in the applied sciences, in engineering, for instance, almost all argumentation relies on specialized warrants.

The matters discussed in this chapter, substance, methodology and argumentation, are some of the things that make inquiry in one discipline quite different from that in another. They affect the intellectual character of each discipline and the way subject matter is handled, discussed and argued about. By tuning in to these things as you do preparatory reading for an assignment, you will prime yourself in the best way possible for the business of writing.

NOTES

1. C. P. Snow, *The Two Cultures: and a Second Look*, 2nd ed. (Cambridge University Press, 1964), pp. 66–68.
2. R. S. Crane, *The Idea of the Humanities*, vol. 1 (University of Chicago Press, 1967), pp. 26–155.
3. W. C. Booth, *Modern Dogma and the Rhetoric of Assent* (University of Chicago Press, 1974).
4. T. S. Kuhn, *The Structure of Scientific Revolutions*, 2nd ed. (University of Chicago Press, 1970).

2

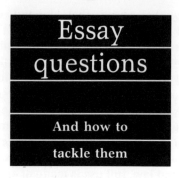

Essay questions

And how to tackle them

Just occasionally students are invited to set their own questions: *Within the field of x, devise a suitably testing question of your own, and answer it magnificently.* But invitations of this sort, like gift blank cheques, don't seem to turn up very often. What could be more desirable when you are slaving away to meet the demands of someone else's question? Unfortunately, inexperienced writers may very well hang themselves in the business of trying to settle on their own subject; and for this reason, among others, most student writing is done in response to questions set by lecturers.

The question or topic or assignment set by the lecturer has built into it some ready-made handles, and by trying your grip on them you can be reasonably sure that you will get the better of the subject, not vice versa. The wording indicates not only what is to be done, but also how, and both explicitly and implicitly communicates the question-setter's intentions. By checking its details you will quickly be able to recognize kinds of questions. There are those that ask you to describe something neutrally, and others that ask you for some kind of judgment about the subject; some that insist that you take a particular attitude as your starting-point, and others that simply plunge you into the midst of a controversy.

Cues on all such possibilities are embedded in three aspects of the wording:
1. the instruction

2. the terminology
3. value-laden words,

and a large part of this chapter will be concerned with them. Looking closely at them is your best guarantee of providing appropriate and relevant material in your answer.

In addition, your response to the question needs to be coordinated. The discussion needs to be focused through a specific proposition so that your writing will have purpose and direction. If you find it hard to formulate a proposition, there are ways of working one out, again using the question as your starting point. Techniques for doing this will be described in the final section of the chapter.

THE INSTRUCTION

Whether it sounds like a cheery invitation or a cold command, any assignment is intended to mobilize you. The instruction may be made explicit in one or more words, or else remain implicit in the total wording. But implicit instructions are most easily examined in the light of the explicit, and so we will begin by discussing the latter. The instruction is often contained in a single instruction word, such as **describe, discuss, outline**, and a limited set of them is used repeatedly in the setting of questions. (A reference list of them is provided at the end of this chapter, on page 23.)

Broadly speaking, instruction words call for two distinct kinds of academic activity. They may ask you to present academic material in a clear, straightforward way, as if you were setting out the facts for someone or explaining them in the generally accepted way; or they may ask you for an individual interpretation or evaluation of certain things, or for an independent argument about them. In the latter cases it is necessary to find a wider context for your material, or to talk about it in relation to some more abstract principles. The first activity we will call exposition/explanation, and the second, interpretation/evaluation/argument. The first activity is the one more frequently required in exams and in writing assignments in the natural sciences, while the latter is probably commoner in the humanities.

But the two activities are interrelated. Interpretive or evaluative questions have to be answered on the basis of facts of some kind, and such writing normally includes some preliminary exposition. We need, therefore, to be able to distinguish the two, as well as to recognize when the question calls for a combination of them.

Some instruction words are relatively unambiguous, and their demands in terms of the two activities are clear. For instance:
1. *Outline the characteristics of biological molecules*
and
2. *Describe and critically evaluate the Malthusian theory of population.*

The words **outline** and **describe** are requests for straight information: please give an exposition of the relevant facts, or explain your understanding of the matter. The second topic, however, asks for more — that you **critically evaluate** the subject also. For this you must look beyond the specified subject (the Malthusian theory of population) to other theories of population and the issues that they raise for the discipline. It is obviously a more searching question.

So far the instruction words themselves have proved helpful in identifying the demands of the question. But unfortunately their meaning can be affected by the specific content of the question or topic, and this is particularly the case with **discuss**, which is probably the most heavily used of all instruction words. Like any well-used word, it has multiple shades of meaning, ranging from something like *describe* to something like *please interpret/evaluate in whatever way you think fit.* Its range of meaning is covered by the following sample topics:
1. *Discuss the interactions that occur between the atmosphere and the oceans.*
2. *Discuss the political ideals of the Roman nobility.*
3. *Discuss the significance of the comic elements in* Romeo and Juliet.

In topic 1, which focuses on physical phenomena, **discuss** is more or less equivalent to **describe**. Topic 2, however, would involve presenting the documentary and institutional evidence as well as some interpretation of it. The most abstract nature of the subject (ideals) makes handling it at least partly a matter of interpretation. In topic 3 the subject is unmistakably a matter for interpretation, and this is confirmed by the fact that **discuss** is coupled with **the significance of**.

In the context of a full sentence, the surrounding words will clarify the demands of the word **discuss**. But there is no such help when **discuss** is appended as a one-word sentence to the end of a quotation. The following is an example of this very common type of topic, taken from the field of law:

The test of foreseeability as developed by the courts has mitigated the harshness of the formerly held principle of virtual strict liability on the part of the tort-feasor. Discuss.

Whether or not we know any law, the openness of the instruction here is clear, and the form of the question appears to leave room for more than one kind of response, depending on the capacity and inclination of the student. The quotation itself focuses attention on changing legal practice and seems to call for a survey of legal history to vindicate or (perhaps) refute the statement. Seen this way, its demands are expository and relatively straightforward. But the topic can also be seen as an invitation to talk about certain principles of law, and interpretation and argument would certainly be involved in handling these more abstract matters. In cases like these we would, before taking up the question, need to consider whether one or other response is more in line with the nature of the course. Instruction words with more than one possible meaning are shown in the reference list (page 23).

Not all assignments embody an explicit instruction, however, and in its absence we must look to the total wording. Quite often it takes the form of a direct question, and through it we may infer the underlying instruction word, again with the help of the reference list:

What are the causes of ageing of the population? . . . OUTLINE, DESCRIBE

What do you understand by the term "money supply"? . . . DEFINE

How did medieval governments obtain the resources to govern? . . . EXPLAIN

How adequately does stratification theory account for inequalities in state socialist countries? . . . EVALUATE

In cases where you still feel unsure as to whether an expository/explanatory or interpretive/evaluative response is required, your best guide is in (a) the specified subject matter, and (b) the typical handling of topics in the course. In the study of English (or any other) literature, interpretation of the subject matter is the regular practice. If you simply describe the contents of a literary work you will be missing the point of the exercise and will perhaps be criticized for "just telling the story". In biology, however, you need to be able to describe exactly what goes on in an organism, and independent interpretation is likely to be criticized as "speculation".

KEY TERMINOLOGY

While the instruction helps to indicate the general demands of the topic, the key terms are always your guide as to the topic's intended scope. Whether technical or non-technical, they designate the phenomena (items, individuals, events, processes, qualities, concepts, etc.) that you are to study, for instance:

causes   ageing of the population
money supply
medieval governments   resources to govern
stratification theory   inequalities   state socialist countries

The key term often amounts to a key phrase, as these examples show. If you can, off the cuff, define the technical terms and paraphase or illustrate the non-technical terms in the topic, you have at least an even chance of being able to handle it in the heat of an exam. Outside exams, of course, you are in the happy position of being able to check up and read up on anything.

When the key words come from ordinary usage, it is often worth checking them in a general dictionary, not simply to confirm your understanding but also as a reminder of the range of meanings that each word may bear. An apparently simple question such as:

Who discovered Australia?
turns very intriguingly on how we take the word **discover**, which in dictionary terms means *to make known something previously unknown.* The discussion could take in quite different kinds of material, depending on whether we took a European or a South-east Asian angle on it.

Likewise, the question:
Were Fascist movements revolutionary?
hangs on more than one sense of the word *revolutionary*, with a possible contrast between Marxist and non-Marxist interpretations of the word.

Unfortunately the key terms of the social and natural sciences don't always appear in the lists of large general dictionaries. Even if they do, they are not likely to be adequately defined for a given discipline. The technical terms of the social sciences are frequently conscripted from common vocabulary, but technical and general meanings of the words will not match exactly, even if there is overlap. Psychological terms such as *anxiety, instinct* and *trauma*, for instance, have much more restricted definitions in psychology than in common usage, and only in a technical dictionary will this be clear. The same is true in areas of the humanities. In literary criticism, such common words as *image, irony* and *tone* are technical terms, and it is a good idea to check their meanings in a glossary of literary terminology.[1]

In the long run the course textbook is really more useful than a technical dictionary, because it not only gives technical definitions of the terms but also presents them in a fuller context. Many terms are not just specialized, but theory-laden, and need to be apprehended in a full theoretical discussion, in relation to other terms in the same theoretical set. For example, the word *superego* can hardly be explained without reference to the terms *id* and *ego*, those other Freudian constructs, and the occurrence of any one of them in a question is, or should be, a reminder to check the Freudian theory in which they are all interrelated. A further problem is that the same terms may be differently used by different theorists (for example, the word *grammar* in linguistics), and this, too, will be clearer in extended readings than in the entries of a technical dictionary. The essential purpose of some assignments is to make you aware of different understandings of the same concept, and scholarly divergences are always worth pointing out. To recognize them suggests intelligent reading!

All the key terms that we have looked at we have in fact used for rather more than just pinpointing our subject. We have exploited them as a way into discussion of the subject and as a guide to the kind of materials or theories we should be looking into. The key terms help to show what range of things is relevant to the topic.

VALUE WORDS

One other type of word is important to the character of a set question — the value word or words. Such words embody a value judgment of some sort, which may be part or virtually all of the word's meaning. It may be positive or negative and may relate to either ethical or aesthetic values that impinge on the subject and must be confronted in responding to the question.

Quite often the key words of the question are themselves value-laden, as in:

Milton's minor poems are **major** *ones,* and

Force *and* **fraud** *are the principal bases of order in human society.*

In each of these, the values in the emphasized words are critical to discussion of the topics concerned. We could not, in discussing Milton's minor poems, sidestep the value judgment expressed in *major* without providing an irrelevant answer. We are obliged to make a value judgment one way or the other, though the criteria on which we base it are entirely of our own choosing. When discussing the principal bases of social order we would have to come to terms with the negatively toned words *force* and *fraud*, which imply general condemnation of whatever practices they are applied to. Those writing on the subject must take the value judgment as their starting point, although they are free to apply it to fewer or more social practices, depending on how many they judge to be reprehensible. Under the heading of *force*, anything from secret police to the obligation to vote (backed up by legally imposed fines) might be included. The selection of examples, and the underlying criteria, are entirely up to the writer.

Thus value words in the topic make it highly likely that some discussion of criteria is called for. (See further, pages 45 to 47.) Handling the topic means deciding why something is good or bad, important or unimportant, in the context of the discipline. The criteria by which you make these judgments and use the value words are (like definitions of key words) the hard core of your discussion. Once you have worked them out it is quite easy to find examples and cases to represent and illustrate them, and the discussion will grow. Naturally, the criteria need to be talked about early in your assignment, so as to tune the reader in to your system of values and ensure that he/she can share your perspective in the ensuing discussion.

WORKING OUT A CENTRAL PROPOSITION

All the points we have mentioned so far will help to guarantee the relevance of what you write about. But we have not yet mentioned the single most vital step in composing any piece of writing, that is, the business of settling on a central proposition. It represents the essence of your response to the set question or topic and should be expressed as a statement in a single sentence. Less than a sentence and you have no point to make; more than a sentence and the point begins to be diffused. Whether the exercise is thousands of words long or only a few hundred, it needs a central proposition to unify the discussion and give purpose to the information offered. Writing that lacks a central proposition is shapeless and frustrating to read. Readers need to know where they are going, and why.

Propositionless writing is usually the result of insufficient thinking about the raw material. Sometimes we have too little that is relevant and desperately stuff everything in; at other times we may just have too much. Either way we may be less than selective about what we include. As Hemingway, among others, has observed, we write the better for what we leave out – not, of course, meaning that shorter is better, but that the process of culling enables us to clarify our intentions with our material. It makes us decide on the principles by which an item should or should not go in. However interesting individual items are for their own sake, they will not "add up" unless they are aligned with the central proposition. Only through that relationship do they take on significance and have real value for the assignment.

The central proposition is something to work at while thinking and reading around the topic. Sometimes the question or topic itself suggests the answering proposition, or sets up clear-cut options. The question:

Does Australia face an energy crisis?

seems to polarize your response, obliging you to respond either with the proposition that:

Australia does indeed face an energy crisis (Yes),

or else

Australia does not face an energy crisis (No).

As in a debate, you are largely relieved of the burden of defining your own position and can simply concentrate on finding data and points to support it. This is not to say that there is no room for an intermediate position. You could, if you preferred, work with some modification of those strong statements about Australia's energy crisis, for instance:

Australia does not face an energy crisis, provided that . . .

But whether thus modified or taken "straight", the proposition implied in the question is a useful starting point.

Many expository and explanatory topics simply point you to a general area of discussion and leave you to supply the specifics. This may not leave you much room to move, however, for only certain specifics can fill the proposition correctly. Unless you know them, you cannot really offer the answering proposition. Thus, when the topic asks you to:

Outline the main effects of waterlogging on soils,

you obviously have to know the right specifics to fill out the answering proposition:

The main effects of waterlogging on soils are x, y and z.

The act of deciding what goes into x, y and z will either help you to write an effective and well-coordinated answer or convince you that it would be better to try another topic. Your freedom to formulate the proposition is very severely constrained in such cases.

There is much more latitude with assignments of the interpretive/evaluative/argumentative kind. They often leave the field wide open for a proposition of the writer's own choosing, and simply indicate a topic area. For example:

Discuss the treatment of social climbing and sexual prudery in the Victorian novel.

Here there is no suggestion as to the kind of proposition expected in reply, and the terms of reference are up to you. But the literary context in which you choose to examine the topic will settle the terms of reference and help you to work out a proposition for your answer. The treatment of social climbing and sexual prudery would have to be discussed in relation to particular novels and novelists, and conventions and individual practices would begin to emerge as soon as you made comparisons. These comparisons would ultimately allow you to make some generalizations about the topic and perhaps to state the proposition that:

Social climbing is represented in a realistic way by a number of Victorian novelists, but sexual prudery by very few.

In the discussion you would, of course, need to specify which novelists did which, and the proposition would coordinate your comments and give them shape and structure.

The same procedure can be readily applied to assignments in any field. Putting the topic in specific contexts always helps to produce the proposition you need. An open topic, such as:

Critically appraise the claim that authoritarianism is a personality variable,

would invite you to test the claim against various theories and experimental studies. Having checked it in the theoretical and empirical literature, you should be able to say, in general terms, how valid it is. A generalization such as:

There is no experimental evidence to support the claim that authoritarianism is a personality variable,

or perhaps:

Authoritarianism can be seen as a personality variable only if we accept x's theory of personality,
could then be formulated.

When the field is wide open, it sometimes takes a little while to capture the generalization you want for the central proposition, and many people recommend trying out tentative ones to see whether they overstate or understate your position. It may prove useful to try to form one in relation to the topic after each piece of reading. By the time you no longer want to modify it you will have a reliable proposition to write to. You will also, incidentally, have digested your reading, and will know exactly where to go for evidence to support the proposition.

This chapter has been concerned with what we might call strategies for handling set questions and topics. Their wording is there to be exploited for indications as to what is expected, although it always pays to look beyond the literal values of the individual words, for many assignments are designed to put you in touch with wider theoretical issues and the values of the discipline. But having a set of strategies like this will help you decide which question out of a list you can best handle, taking full account of their individual demands and, in exams, the present state of your knowledge.

Having selected the question, assessed its demands and worked out the essence of a response, we move on to the matter of organization and the laying out of our material. The organization of expository/explanatory writing is somewhat different from that of the interpretive/evaluative/argumentative kind, and will therefore be treated in two separate chapters.

TABLE 1

REFERENCE LIST OF COMMONLY USED INSTRUCTION WORDS

account for	give an explanation as to why
analyse	1. examine closely
	2. examine x in terms of its components and show how they interrelate
assess	decide the value of
compare	discuss x and y in terms of their similarities and differences
contrast	discuss x and y, emphasizing their differences
define	1. explain (make clear) what is meant by
	2. use a definition or definitions to explore the concept of
describe	present an account of
discuss	1. make x your subject
	2. consider and offer some interpretation or evaluation of
enumerate	give an item-by-item account of
evaluate	attempt to form a judgment about
examine	inspect and report on in detail
explain	1. make clear the details of
	2. show the reason for or underlying cause of, or the means by which
illustrate	offer an example or examples to
	1. show how/that
	2. make concrete the concept of
indicate	focus attention on
outline	go through the main features of
prove	show by logical argument
review	1. report the chief facts about
	2. offer a critique of
summarize	describe concisely

NOTES
1. See, for example, M. H. Abrams, *A Glossary of Literary Terms* (Holt, Rinehart and Winston, New York, 1971).

3

Writing to inform

Expository essays

Explanatory essays

When talking informally with anyone, the information we offer is always affected by their presence. Even when there is a lot to tell, we normally avoid delivering it in a long, uninterrupted spiel, like the archetypal salesman or preacher. Rather, we communicate a chunk at a time, making sure after each that our listener is with us and prepared to hear more. The chunks are composed on the run, leaving gaps and creating overlaps, and we may have to discontinue the subject before covering it fully. We must continually adapt and restructure our communication in response to the needs and demands of the audience.

Writing frees us from some of these pressures. There is no need to work on the run, and time is not a pressing problem (at least it is more a matter of calendar-watching than clock-watching). Time, or rather *space* in which to communicate our subject, is guaranteed by the quota of words allotted to the assignment. In that space the subject can develop its own shape and momentum.

Yet because we *do* write in long, continuous stretches, we must give particular thought to the structuring of ideas and information. Spontaneous writing from most people's pens produces a turbulent "stream of consciousness", which makes turgid reading for anyone else. To communicate our ideas we must control their presentation, and this means:

1. deciding what are the independent points, or units of information, we have to convey

and

2. arranging them in an appropriate order, or hierarchy.

Between them, these two operations will suggest a scheme for presentation that aids both writer and reader. Research confirms that the reader's understanding of a text depends very much on being able to relate its substance to a familiar cognitive pattern or scheme.[1] So the scheme not only provides access for the reader but can also ensure that things are read as the writer intended.

A scheme is indispensable, though that is not to say that all writing begins with a scheme. Quite often writers find it impossible to begin that way – their minds seem to go stiff at the thought – and mental cramps can be eased by simply starting to write in an *un*schematized way, aiming first only to produce a flow of ideas on paper. This is sometimes called **writer-based prose** – an ego-centred prose that does not aim to project ideas to the reader.[2] It helps to get anything down. As you harness your thoughts on paper, they will begin to move and to lead somewhere. By the end of a page (or even a paragraph) you will find you suddenly recognize what the assignment has to say and do. The page itself should be thrown away, but the points that emerged will enable you to start planning. You will know what there is to discuss and begin to see the headings under which the assignment can take shape. Those headings will help to suggest a scheme for presenting your material.

Whether you approach it through writer-based prose or not, a scheme needs to be found for every assignment. Several kinds of schemes are illustrated in this chapter. Although the actual schemes used vary with the nature of the writer's subject, they fall into just a few groups, based on such things as time, causation or generality. In what follows, the schemes are grouped under two broad headings: (1) natural, and (2) artificial. The first group includes those schemes that reflect relationships in the real world; the second, those that are imposed by the writer.

An awareness of the various types of scheme will help you to pick the one most suitable for your material. The schemes described are useful for both expository and explanatory questions, that is, those which ask *what*, as well as those which ask *how* or *why*. The approach to *how* and *why* assignments is, however, slightly more complicated, and they are given special attention towards the end of the chapter (page 35 ff.) under the heading "Explaining how and why".

NATURAL SCHEMES based on *time, process* or *cause-and-effect*
Time is probably the most fundamental of all organizing principles. The sense of things being ordered in a time sequence is basic to our perception of everyday happenings, and when reading we tend to respond to a text along those lines until given cause to think otherwise.[3] It is a scheme by default. Time ordering therefore communicates very readily to the reader, and is worth capitalizing on if your material permits.

In the natural sciences you may well be concerned with an instance of growth and/or change in the context of natural time, as in assignments such as:

Outline the life cycle of the malarial mosquito
Write an essay on chromosomal evolution in any plant group of your choice
Discuss the young child's acquisition of speech sounds.

The first of these assignments involves clear-cut stages of development and a firm order of occurrence:

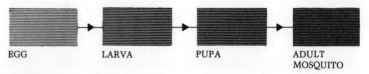

EGG   LARVA   PUPA   ADULT MOSQUITO

FIGURE 1: *A time-based scheme*

In this case a **time-based scheme** is the obvious choice. It is also useful for the second and third assignments above, even though the sequences involved in them are less clear-cut — in the second because the stages of chromosomal evolution are less easy to differentiate, and in the third because there are alternative orders of acquisition after the first consonant and vowel. The differences and alternatives are still most effectively explored in a firm chronological context.

Historical time rather than natural time can often provide a context for the study of society and human thought. Again it helps writers to structure their subject matter as well as to highlight development and change. It incidentally tends to suggest progress towards the present status quo, an effect which is handy if you want a climax but unfortunate if you don't. If you are tracing the history of a social institution, for example, or developments in economic or educational theory, and you feel that things have become decadent or less enlightened in the course of time, the downward direction will need to be stressed. With this small proviso, a time-based scheme is widely useful, for instance in tasks like:

Examine the historical bases of racism in Australia
or
    Describe the form of the English dictionary in its first century and a half.

The latter invites you to trace the evolution of the dictionary through such stages as:

- the "hard words" list (Cawdrey, 1604)
- first regular etymologies (Blount, 1656)
- everyday words in word list (Kersey, 1702)
- citations to support definitions (Johnston, 1755),

and these suggest both the units of your discussion and their order of presentation.

A time-based scheme has the advantage of interrelating the individual sections of an essay and at the same time providing a backbone for the whole. It is a good one to implement in exam writing because it communicates through the very sequence of material and does not, like other schemes (especially the artificial ones), depend on explicit identification at regular intervals. If in the heat of the moment you forgot to mention the relative timing of a particular stage, its place would still be clear in the overall sequence. The scheme is maintained implicitly.

Many of the advantages of the time-based scheme belong also to the **process-based** scheme. The processes involved are sequences or patterns of forces – physical, chemical, mechanical, etc. – that can be predicted in relation to a particular outcome. Trace through the process step-by-step and you have a reliable scheme for your subject. It is the verbal equivalent of a flow chart. Process schemes are particularly helpful for the science student and lend themselves to many an exam question in both pure and applied science. For example:

Discuss the mode of action of organophosphate insecticides
Describe the breakdown of proteins to amino acids in mammalian digestion
Give an account of the features associated with the engineering stress/strain curve.

The first two topics both centre on chemical processes, and these would provide schemes for each answer. The layout of the mammalian digestive tract suggests a supplementary (or alternative) scheme for the second one. The third depends on a more abstract process, the progressive changes in the shape of a substance such as a piece of metal as it has to bear progressive increases in load. The relationships would appear thus on a graph:

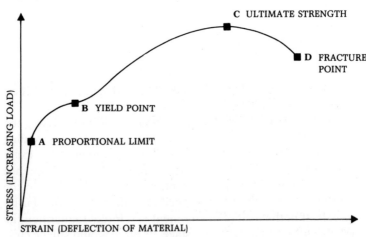

FIGURE 2: *A graph of the engineering stress/strain curve*

A written account of the engineering stress/strain curve would follow the sequence from A to D, tracing the distortion in the shape of the material through to breaking point.

One further type of scheme, that of **cause-and-effect**, is as useful in the humanities and social sciences as in the natural sciences. A cause-and-effect scheme is often possible when one of those two words appears in the wording of the topic, and often also with other words that imply some sort of contingent relationship, for example, *affect, consequence, control, depend, determine, influence, result*. However, not all assignments embodying such words actually centre on the interrelationship of cause and effect. In the following:

What were the underlying causes of World War II?
What are the consequences of ageing of the population?

the focus is simply on causes or effects, not how they interrelate, and the writer needs something other than a cause-and-effect scheme to present them with (perhaps a time-based scheme, or one of the artificial schemes discussed below). But when both causes and effects are to be examined in the assignment, the obvious scheme is also the best one on which to base our presentation. Examples of this, from geology and literature, are:

Outline the effects of the climatic changes of the last 20 000 years on the land forms of eastern Australia
Discuss the characteristics of the English morality play that influenced the staging of Elizabethan plays.

Handling these assignments requires you first to decide on relevant causes or conditioning factors. These, when coupled with their particular consequences, form a set of units on which to base your presentation. (See figure 3, for example.)

If the answer revolves around a single cause-and-effect unit, it provides all the scheme you will need for writing it up. But whenever there are two or more cause-and-effect units like the one diagrammed above, further schematic planning will be needed to order or rank those units. The literature assignment would call for a comprehensive scheme (probably an artificial one) to give order to the individual cause-and-effect units within it.

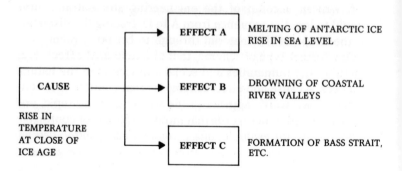

FIGURE 3: A cause-and-effect scheme

ARTIFICIAL SCHEMES based on *generality, importance, comparison*, or *problem and solution*

When there are no natural relationships of time or process or causation underlying your subject matter, they will need to be set out according to a specially imposed ordering principle, which we will call an **artificial scheme**. In an artificial scheme the relationship between one unit of material and another is in the eye of the beholder. This might suggest infinite numbers of schemes varying with all the individuality of human perception, but, as with the natural schemes, they boil down to just a few groups.

A scheme based on **generality** is often used to present a body of conceptual material, for instance when we are asked to describe an academic principle or theory. Perhaps the task is to explain (in the expository sense: see EXPLAIN 1 in table 1, page 23) a theory of the origin of the universe, or Plato's theory of art, or the theory of price determination, or Chomsky's theory of language competence . . . Whatever it is, much the best way to present it is to begin with the broadest or most fundamental idea in the theory (normally its most general principle) and to move from there to secondary or more particular matters. Having the broadest statement first helps to indicate the whole domain of the theory as well as to set up a firm context for the particular details.

To take the last as our example. We might begin to describe Chomsky's theory of language competence by stating his fundamental assumption that language is a set of rules (that is, *grammar*) internalized by every adult native speaker. This premise is the logical basis for a number of other tenets in Chomskyan theory:

- that their internalized grammars allow native speakers to create correctly formed sentences quite freely;
- that the internalized grammar enables the native speaker to interpret and judge the correctness of sentences never previously heard . . .

and so on.

A general-to-particular scheme works rather like an inverted triangle, with the broadest principle as its base:

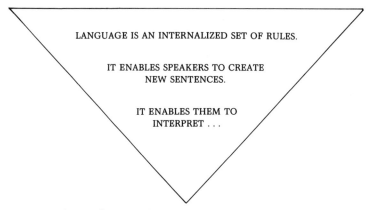

FIGURE 4: *A general-to-particular scheme*

An inverted triangle or pyramid is, of course, the structural shape used by journalists in the ordinary reporting of events. They use the base of the pyramid to state the essential fact about the event, and then add other, progressively more specialized details. It is a strategy to allow the editor to take as much or as little of the article as he has space for without losing the key points. Students writing exam papers find themselves up against a similar problem, wanting to ensure that they have discussed at least the core of the topic before time runs out. The inverted triangle helps to guarantee this, even if you have to break off before the planned end point.

A similar strategy helps in assignments that ask you to report the most important (chief, main) facts or factors in a topic. If you arrange your topic units in a scale of relative *importance* you will have an orderly scheme by which to present them, even if the units themselves are like chalk and cheese, and are hard to relate in any other way. The scale of importance often comes to the rescue when no other scheme suggests itself. Whether your task is to talk about techniques for assessing crop damage and loss, or strengthening polymers, or factors that impeded the development of industrial democracy in Australia, or themes in Shakespeare's sonnets, you should be able to rank your subject units in order of importance, starting with the most important and working down to the less important.

In describing the themes of Shakespeare's sonnets, for instance, you might observe that one theme – time and time-lessness – occurs in many, while other themes are more occa-sional. So you would be justified in treating the time theme as the most important. In an exam answer you would probably begin with this and, according to the inverted triangle strategy, cover as many of the less common themes as you could. Out-side exams, however, when not writing against the clock, you might well use the opposite strategy, identifying first some of the lesser themes and working up to the dominant one.

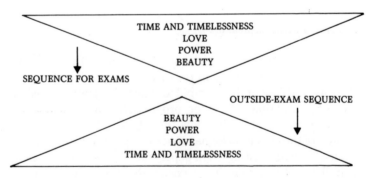

FIGURE 5: Scale-of-importance schemes

The outside-exam sequence allows you to develop a kind of climax with your most significant unit, and it makes effective reading. The sequence would not necessarily work well with all kinds of subject matter, however. If the task was to discuss techniques for strengthening polymers, the rhetorical effect of climax would be poor compensation for delaying your discussion of the most important technique.

A **comparative scheme** is quite commonly invited by the wording of a topic, though responding to the invitation is not really a straightforward matter. Of course there will be two distinct targets (or groups of them) to compare, for example:

the crises of the fourteenth and seventeenth centuries
the economic institutions of market socialism and the Soviet system of control planning and management
the musical styles of Debussy and Ravel.

But this does not necessarily mean that you should spend the first half of your essay on, say, Debussy, and the second on Ravel. It all depends on the kind of comparison you are aiming at: whether it is to be holistic, or based on a limited set of criteria. The criteria, or points for comparison, are not often spelt out in the topic and are usually left for you to decide on. If you have a set of points on which to compare your two subjects, your scheme might well be to proceed by introducing each point individually, relating it to first one subject and then the other.

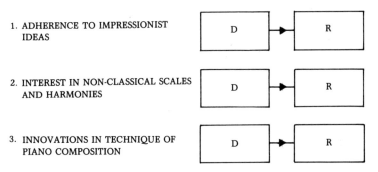

FIGURE 6: *A point-by-point comparison scheme*

This scheme makes efficient and precise comparisons. But it is not the ideal way to communicate the overall distinctive character of your two targets. If your aim is to offer a holistic comparison (or if it is difficult to find parallel points to compare) then you would prefer a scheme that gives all attention to first one target and then the other.

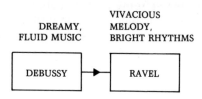

FIGURE 7: A block comparison scheme

The distinctly different quality of the two composers' music could be more fully communicated this way.

One further type of scheme may help to organize the material in an expository assignment: the **solution**. This scheme lends itself to discussions about ways of handling physical problems, which are often called for in the applied sciences; for example:

horizontal distance measuring
fastening partial dentures
reducing rolling in ships.

Although the topic normally focuses on the solving of the problem (and indeed often asks for more than one kind of solution) it is worthwhile devoting some space to the problem itself. The answer will then consist of two complementary parts; and a preliminary account of the problem gives point to the solution or solutions you describe.

A problem-solution scheme can sometimes be effective in the discussion of more abstract problems, for instance in education or social work. In law, problem-solution, or problem-*resolution*, is at the heart of a common training exercise, in which students must sort out the legal consequences of the "facts" in a contrived "case", and recognize and deal with any ambiguities in the relevant law.

EXPLAINING HOW AND WHY

The topics discussed so far in this chapter have been straight expository ones, ones that identify a subject (or sometimes two) for you to talk about, but leave it to you to decide on a way to assemble and present your material. Whatever scheme you used would help to structure your units of material for the reader, and incidentally indicate a particular relationship between them (as of time, process, etc.). That relationship would not be the centre of attention, however.

But when asked to explain *how* or *why*, your task is to find a set of coherent relationships in your subject matter. The organizing schemes we have been examining represent just such relationships, and you will be able to base your explanations upon them.

The particular kind of explanation is broadly indicated by *how* or *why*, *how* questions being concerned with the means whereby certain things are achieved, and *why* questions with underlying causes and reasons, or sometimes the justification for a given practice. But there are no simple equations, and the explanatory line needs to be dictated by the subject matter itself. To find a suitable explanatory line for the assignment, you may care to turn your *how* or *why* question into one or more *what* questions. This exercise shows up the type of material you will be handling as you develop your explanation. It also shows up the different perspectives of expository and explanatory assignments.

Let us put this into practice in an explanatory question, such as:

> *How do deserts form at low, medium and high latitudes respectively?*

Reworded as an expository assignment, the question might be:

> *What factors contribute to the formation of deserts at . . ?*

This is not, of course, the question set, but its wording may well help you in your thinking about the assignment. It serves to identify more precisely the kind of substance you will be concerned with: factors, climatic and geographical. And in thinking about them you will probably see a relationship among them − that of process − which would give you an explanatory line to work with. There are, of course, both "hot" and "cold" deserts, formed by different configurations of the key variables, including temperature and precipitation. But the key variables make up a set that you could usefully present in **process** terms.

How assignments in literature and the arts are often concerned with artistic technique, asking you to discuss the means by which an author obtains certain effects. For example:

How does Peter Weiss make exciting theatre of the political issues represented in Marat/Sade?

Explain how Pope's use of rhymed verse influences the reader's response to his subject.

In each of these there are two kinds of variables to discuss, which emerge if you try to reword them as *what* questions. The latter assignment, for instance, involves:

(a) *What uses does Pope put rhymed verse to?*

and

(b) *What responses does Pope evoke in his reader?*

The points to be discussed under (a), such as the special emphasis and the contrastive force attached to rhymed words, have to be related to their effect noted under (b), in particular the sense of comedy and satire. These effects probably depend on the incongruity perceived in Pope's material, and this incongruity is cleverly underscored by the contrastive force of certain rhymed words. Thus there is a contingent relationship between the use of rhyme and the responses evoked in the reader.[4] **Cause-and-effect** is therefore a suitable explanatory line to exploit in an answer to this question.

In *why* questions, the writer's task is to explain the cause or underlying reason for something, and, as you might expect, the cause-and-effect approach is useful in handling the more straightforward of them, for example, *Why is a clear sky blue?* But the more complex the question (the more variables involved) the more likely it is that some other kind of relationship would help the explanatory answer. This can be seen in another scientific question:

Why do most large animals move more slowly than most small animals?

The question involves two other kinds of question:

(a) *By what means do animals move?*

and

(b) *What factors make small bodies more mobile than large ones?*

While question (a) highlights similarities, question (b) would bring out differences, and this suggests that a **comparative** approach would in this case yield an effective explanation.

Now a question from the social sciences:

Why are the benefits of collective rural organization so rarely realized?

The assignment spotlights the difficulties and problems of a particular rural system, and it is easy enough to frame the associated *what* questions:

What are the benefits of collective rural organization?

and

What problems arise with collective rural organization?

Though the assignment encourages you to look at the problems, it evidently doesn't expect you to find solutions, and a problem-solution approach would not work. More appropriate to the question would be an explanation that examines the problems in an order of magnitude, leading up to the most intractable. The explanatory line would then underscore the insoluble character of the problem, and the answer would be both reasonable and rhetorically effective.

Finally, let us consider the *why* question that concerns neither means nor causes, but asks us to justify a particular practice:

Why is simulation a widely used tool in operations research?

The assignment involves the questions:

What are the applications of simulation?

and

What advantages does simulation offer the operations researcher?

Here, again, the second of our supplementary questions helps to suggest an effective explanatory approach. Simulation solves a number of the basic problems confronting operations research, and so a **problem-solution** approach here would satisfy the question very well.

This chapter has shown how schemes serve to structure material for discussion as well as provide a basis for explanation, where this is required. They are all you need for expository or explanatory questions, particularly those set in exams to test your knowledge of the subject matter of the discipline. But such questions also come up outside exams, for instance in tutorial papers in which you must hold forth on a particular topic or theoretical viewpoint to your fellow students. Even more importantly, the schemes are often needed as structural devices within interpretive/evaluative/argumentative assignments, to which we will now turn.

NOTES

1. G. Dillon, *Constructing Texts* (Indiana University Press, Bloomington, 1981) p. 53.
2. L. Flower and J. Hayes, *Problem-Solving Strategies for Writers* (Harcourt, Brace, Jovanovich, New York, 1981) pp. 147–57.
3. Dillon, pp. 61–63.
4. These assignments (like the interpretive ones of the next chapter) depend on your defining a response to the work, but they imply that there is a consensus on this, which you can treat as established fact. For the purposes of such questions, that response is an objective phenomenon, just like the deserts of the question on page 35.

4

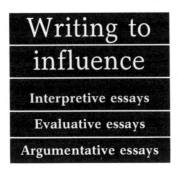

Writing to influence

Interpretive essays

Evaluative essays

Argumentative essays

The writing we talked about in chapter 4 was geared to the business of conveying information to the reader. Many of the topics were of the "stand and deliver" type (often found in exams), which put you on the spot and ask you to present the facts or explain your understanding of a standard subject. The same questions outside exams are a little like writing an article for an encyclopedia, where the writer concentrates on the established core of knowledge on a given subject. In the article the writer may acknowledge controversial aspects of the subject and minority views, but avoids taking sides. Such writing deals with information that is as reliable and certain as any human knowledge can be at a particular point in time.

Not all that students write about is in the realm of (relative) certainty. In fact much of it is in the realms of probability and possibility, and the art of writing becomes that of making the most convincing case you can from a patchy or slippery base of information. Aristotle distinguished between four kinds of discourse on grounds of the relative certainty of the substance they dealt with:

(a) scientific   certain[1]
(b) dialectical   probable
(c) rhetorical   seemingly probable
(d) poetic   internally probable.

Aristotle's use of the word "scientific" was broader than ours, roughly equivalent to non-fiction, and would have embraced writing in subjects as various as those covered in chapter 3. The word "poetic" was also broader, referring to creative literature generally, and goes beyond the concerns of this book. But the **dialectical** and **rhetorical** discourse that he identified (meaning, respectively, writing that explores a process of logical reasoning and writing that presents a view persuasively) are exactly the kinds to be discussed in this chapter, although we will examine them under three rather than two headings.

The underlying aim of all the writing discussed in this chapter is to influence the reader. It is not the type of influence suggested in Dale Carnegie's *How to Win Friends and Influence People*, which involves exercising a force of personality, but influence of a more intellectual type, intended to affect the thinking of the reader. It obliges the reader to recognize the soundness of the view or position we hold (whether or not it alters his/her deepest convictions). We cannot offer any absolute certainties. But we can hope to show the reasonableness of our view by offering grounds for accepting it and by selecting information that bears it out.

Selecting information is crucial to the art of writing-to-influence. Information at large has little value, firstly because it is always incomplete and secondly because it does not help to pinpoint a particular view. This is why beginning students in literature and history are warned "not to tell the story". But a careful selection of literary or historical data from your sources will both clarify the view and help to justify it to the reader.

We will be looking at three kinds of writing-to-influence: **interpretive**, **evaluative**, and **argumentative**. The interpretive involves taking a particular descriptive perspective on your material; the evaluative, forming a judgment; and the argumentative, examining the grounds for accepting or rejecting a particular proposition. For the sake of clarity and convenience they will be discussed separately, though they can certainly be used in combination. You may pass from interpretation to evaluation, for instance, in a discussion of D. H. Lawrence's symbols, or use an interpretation of data to underpin your argumentative proposition (see page 49). But even in "mixed" writing, one of the three modes normally dominates, hence the broad classifications on which this chapter is based.

One further point to note: the wording of the assignment does not necessarily make it interpretive or evaluative or argumentative. Some assignments can be tackled in more than one way, depending on your inclinations and the materials at your disposal. A question such as: *Is homosexuality a symptom of an underlying illness, or a normal variant of human sexuality?* could be taken as an interpretive exercise (What does it mean to claim it is an illness?), or as an argumentative exercise (What bodies of evidence are there to support the proposition that it is one or the other?). You might choose to influence your reader by either means. The labels **interpretive/evaluative/argumentative** should be seen as a chosen way of handling the assignment, not a categorization of the question or topic itself.

INTERPRETIVE WRITING

So far we have simply said that interpretation is a descriptive activity, and it is time to define it more closely. Interpretation is a form of analysis which highlights a particular meaning or thematic emphasis in an artistic work, or which recognizes trends or patterns in data in history, politics, sociology, economics, etc. It aims to characterize the raw material generally, though it uses a particular focus.

An interpretation is *one* way of viewing the data, one among others possible. The simplest group of lines may set up more than one perspective (and shapes either concave or convex), and artists such as Escher exploit this ambiguity to force us to construe their drawings in more than one way. In any complex body of verbal or visual data there is scope for alternative interpretations. They may diverge considerably, as when one viewer declares that Alain Renais' film *Providence* (1977) is about fiction and reality, and another, with equal conviction, that it is about father-and-son relationships. Similarly, the struggle over miners' licences in the gold rush period could be viewed as a matter of law and order, or provisional income tax, or keeping rural labour down on the farm. Any of these interpretations could be shown to be viable. One view may be more widely shared than others, but if the others can be justified from the data, there is no reason why they should not be advanced.

The interpretations just mentioned are all vested in a key phrase or set of words,[2] for example, *fiction and reality*, or *father-and-son relationships*. That key will be the touchstone of the assignment, expressing the essence of the view, marking the theme of your discussion and helping to select relevant material. Interpretations may also be vested in a classic model or theory,[3] and the model then provides a framework for the discussion. To illustrate this let us go back to the goldminer's licence and formulate an interpretation of it as an instrument of the land-owning classes for maintaining the balance of power against the rural work force. This interpretation of course appeals to the Marxist theory of class struggle to account for the licence problem, and it would have to be justified by identifying the classic variables of Marxist analysis (such as bourgeois profiteering and an exploited proletariat) in the historical context. A model-based interpretation requires you to find a particular complex of variables in the data and to show that they interact in a predictable way.

Ready-made interpretations are often given in assignment topics to see what you make of them. They may be outrageous or more-or-less reasonable, and you must use your knowledge of the data (and of any model appealed to) to decide. If the interpretation seems reasonable and your reaction is just to say *yes* to it, you simply have to find a battery of examples to support it. At other times you may want to say *yes, up to a point*, and your answer will fall into two parts, firstly, data that conforms to the interpretation, and, secondly, some that is not amenable. A qualified answer like this is sometimes necessitated by the question when it begins: *How far . . . ?* or *To what extent . . ?* In a *qualified yes* answer you have more room to exercise your discretion than in a *straight yes* answer and can show off your ability to interpret your material independently. This is even more true when you write to refute an interpretation entirely with a resounding *no*. There you must not only explain what is wrong with the given interpretation, but also substitute and justify one of your own.

Let us now look at three interpretive assignments, which answer with:

(a) a **straight yes**
(b) a **qualified yes**
(c) a **no**.

When you respond with a **straight yes** to an interpretive question, the biggest problem is managing your material. Your response is probably based on the conviction that almost all the evidence points that way, and so you will have to take care to be selective with all the things that spring to mind. A history question such as:

Did Europe develop a superiority complex with regard to the rest of the world during the colonial era?

draws a vigorous affirmative response from most people, and there are many kinds of evidence to justify it. The superior attitude is expressed in familiar clichéd phrases, such as "darkest Africa" and its "benighted souls", and in a vast number of documented comments on the inferiority of the arts, religion, technology and administrative practices of non-European peoples. This explicit evidence starts to mount up before we have even begun to assemble all the non-documentary evidence, all the colonial practices and institutions that embodied it implicitly.

But even when all the evidence points your way, you should still be selective. With a wide range to choose from, you can pick the most striking examples in each category, and the process of selecting strengthens your case in two ways. It will yield a set of consistently convincing pieces of evidence (which is of no small importance if you aim to influence your reader's thinking), and it encourages you to recognize and use a variety of evidence (for example, the explicit/implicit and their sub-categories, described in the previous paragraph). These different kinds of evidence will of course serve as structural units for your essay.

Now, an assignment that invites a **qualified yes** response. The example chosen asks you to use a familiar economic model in discussing a socio-political issue, but suggests that the model will have only limited applicability:

Examine the extent to which economic supply-and-demand analysis can be applied to military manpower.

The essay would fall into three sections of unequal size. Clearly you would need first to present some exposition of the supply-and-demand model of resources, drawing attention to its characteristic relationships, but not at too great length. The features of the model would then need to be applied to the matter of military manpower, with some considerable time spent comparing military and market resources. While the second section would highlight where the "market" model proved a useful interpretive aid, the third would draw attention to those aspects of military manpower that were not adequately or suitably represented in the model. The relative sizes of the second and third sections would probably reflect the extent to which you felt the model could be applied.

Finally, let us look at a case where **No!** seems the only possible answer. The interpretation offered in a question may provoke you to a strong reaction either because it is deliberately inappropriate, or because it is sited in the midst of a controversy where interpretations tend to polarize. Either way, you need a good command of the raw material to refute the given interpretation and replace it with your own.

The following literature assignment centres on a strongly worded interpretation of Shakespeare's *Macbeth*:

"This dead butcher" . . . Do you agree with Malcolm's description of Macbeth?

Malcolm's word *butcher* is likely to seem objectionable to anyone who has seen the play unfold. Macbeth is unquestionably guilty of murder, but the killing takes place in a context that makes it neither unmotivated nor devoid of remorse. Shakespeare makes it clear that Macbeth was motivated by a complex of human and supernatural forces, and his ambition to become king of Scotland develops amid inter-clan rivalry over the succession. Our knowledge of Macbeth's motives, as well as our awareness of his sense of guilt, makes us disinclined to see him simply as a slaughterman.

Examining the defects of the given interpretation leads us on to what seems a more appropriate interpretation. It takes shape

out of our objections, out of our feeling that Macbeth is charac-
terized in a remarkably human way, as *a man tempted and
betrayed by an ambition*. A set of words like this would articulate the interpretation we wish to offer instead of the one given
and serve as a key for the rest of the discussion. What we have
in fact done is devise a solution to a perceived problem, and
a problem-solution scheme (see page 34) suggests itself as a
structure for the essay. Both parts of the essay would be closely
linked with the actual substance of the play (since we have used
it to reject one interpretation and to distil another); and with
such justification our case has the best chance of influencing
the reader's thinking.

EVALUATIVE WRITING

In both interpretive and evaluative writing we are trying to "sell"
a point of view. But while interpretation is a neutral activity,
claiming to describe the raw material by means of an appropriate key, evaluation is deliberately judgmental.

Your purpose in evaluative writing is to show how you
formed your value judgment, and to justify it. It depends on
two things:

(a) an explanation of the criterion or criteria (that is, the
    yardstick or principles) to be used, and
(b) systematic application of the criterion/criteria to the
    raw material.

The criteria chosen are all-important for the structure and
coherence of evaluative writing. Your evaluation cannot be
shared unless the reader understands the criterion/criteria on
which it is based. The reader needs to know the grounds on
which you judge *Nostromo* to be Conrad's most successful
novel, rather than any other; and only by setting forth your
criteria can you justify your choice and show it is not arbitrary
or idiosyncratic. The criteria you work with normally set up
scales on which your material will rate more or less highly,
and you can compare one block of material with another against
the same scale or yardstick. The scales that underlie evaluations in the humanities are usually qualitative, differentiating
things only broadly, in such terms as *high/medium/low* or

good/fair/poor, etc. In the natural sciences and the quantitative social sciences, the scales are frequently numerical, and could be envisaged in terms of graphs or histograms, etc. (see pages 62 to 66).

In evaluating anything you may use one or more criteria, and there are examples of each to follow. Multiple criteria are usually involved when the assignment leads students into areas of professional decision-making, for example in medicine, engineering, architecture, law, where they must exercise evaluative skills on a particular case. But before getting on to such pre-professional evaluations, let us look at some evaluations of a purely academic kind, which may be called for in any tertiary-level discipline.

Evaluations in academic areas are often vested in words of rather fuzzy connotations, such as *effective, important, interesting, significant, successful, valuable.*[4] Out of context, as this list shows, they have little meaning, and what meaning they seem to have in a phrase or sentence is borrowed from surrounding words. The qualities of an important poem bear little resemblance to the qualities of an important general. The most certain thing about each of those words is that the writers using them want to commend something to our attention. The words stake out a claim without really detailing it. The central task in evaluative writing is therefore setting out the grounds or criteria against which you would use the evaluative word.

Evaluations, like interpretations, are an individual response, and in both, widely differing responses can usually be justified. Because the justification is the most important thing, an assignment may be left very open, like the following (actually from economics):

What is the most interesting fact you have learned in this course? Why do you deem it to be so?

How and where you apply the word *interesting* are gloriously unrestricted here – which is not to say you should use an excessively personal criterion, as in "I have a taste for the exotic!". Clearly you are expected to evaluate your chosen fact in the context of other things learned in the course and to formulate some academic criterion by which it stands out, as (a) the least predictable, or (b) the most far-reaching, perhaps. If you decide the latter, you could review the course material in terms of the breadth or narrowness of the concepts presented, rather as in the general-to-particular scheme discussed above (pages 30 to 32). The scale suggested by your criterion often, as in this case, suggests a scheme by which to structure your essay.

In more typical assignments the target to be evaluated is indicated, and the choice of criteria is less open. But there is still some room for individuality, as in the following biology question:

Which group of vertebrates is in your opinion the most success-ful? Justify your answer.

Your justification might depend on one or more criteria of success:

(a) sheer numbers of species
(b) world distribution of the species
(c) adaptation to different climates
(d) survival through geological time . . . etc.

Were you to use all those it could prove difficult to limit the range of contenders for the title. But if you work only with interrelated criteria, such as world distribution of the species and its adaptability, it should be possible to single out the most successful. In presenting your answer, you would want to compare your most successful group with others less successful, and your criteria would offer you points of comparison by which to structure your essay. (Cf. pages 33 to 34.)

Evaluative writing is a tool of both academic and professional inquiry, as we said earlier. In the professionally oriented disciplines of a university or college, the criteria by which you evaluate a case are again all-important, although they usually form an established set that you are expected to work with. Your problem is not deciding on them, but balancing their often conflicting demands.

A conflict of interests is particularly acute in such a discipline as architecture, where practical and aesthetic considerations often clash head on. Buildings must be designed to facilitate all the activities of their occupants, and be structurally sound and visually attractive as well. It is not so easy to achieve all objectives. The problem may be put before later-year students in the following form:

Discuss the advantages and disadvantages of space structures. Your discussion should cover the following points:

(a) forms of space structures
(b) their uses
(c) structural analysis and geometry
(d) fabrication with special regard to joints
(e) erection
(f) aesthetics.

It is a sizable list of considerations, but a good example of the variety of things that architects must take into account when making professional decisions. The ultimate professional judgment comes from an ability to harmonize all those things.

Pre-professional assignments are set in many quarters of the applied sciences, as well as business management and law. Further examples, from (a) psychiatry, and (b) law, follow:

(a) *A general practitioner is often asked for a prescription for a psychotropic drug. Discuss how you would evaluate a request for a sedative-hypnotic drug and a request for an anti-depressant drug, specifying the criteria on which you would or would not meet these requests.*

(b) *Critically analyse the decision in* Cameron *v.* Hogan *(1934) 51 CLR 358 and assess its value as a precedent in Australia today.*

Neither of these topics mentions the actual criteria to be used. Knowing which apply in a particular case is obviously part of the training. Such assignments test students' familiarity with the context of professional decision-making and their ability to form sound evaluations within them.

ARGUMENTATIVE WRITING

Argumentative writing is probably what most people think of first when there is talk of writing-to-influence. But some rather different kinds of language get called **argumentative**, so we must first clarify what we mean by that word. At its heart is the word *argument*, which itself contributes to the variety because it means different things when we say (a) *people are having an argument*, and when we say (b) *a person hasn't got an argument.* In sense (a), *argument* equals "dispute" or "quarrel", and from this **argumentative** can mean something like "apt to dispute and debate in a rather inflexible way". But *argument* in sense (b) means "a logical reason, or a set of them, which can combine to support a proposition". (See pages 19 to 22, on propositions.) In speaking of argumentative writing we will be drawing on this latter use of *argument* and will be thinking of writing that is supported and structured by a set of reasons.

Argumentative writing relies on an infrastructure of reasons. The writer may argue on the strength of notions warranted by common consensus (see pages 8 to 11, on warrants) and/or with generalizations from the data. Relatively few argumentative assignments depend *just* on the latter, but they do occur in the form of speculative questions in those that ask you to apply a generalized set of historical circumstances to another hypothetical context. For instance:

(a) *If Hitler were to return to Germany during this decade, could he exercise power as he did fifty years ago?*

(b) *"The Peterloo massacre could only have happened in Manchester." Discuss.*

Both the assignments ask you to generalize about the circumstances of a historical phenomenon, in (a), about the conditions that helped Hitler rise to power, and the constitutional factors that gave him free rein; and in (b), the social pressures of the early Industrial Revolution in Manchester. You then have to transfer those generalizations in the case of (a) to a later historical context, and in the case of (b) to other urban contexts, to see if they apply there too. Although the argument arises out of specific historical data, the details become eclipsed in the generalizations you make, and those generalizations are the pillars of your argument.

Argumentative writing often draws on common assumptions as well as generalizations from the data. Both help to define the kind of expectations we can reasonably have about a particular subject, and the position we can most reasonably hold in realms where there are no certainties. The predictions on which government social and economic policy is based have to be made this way. The following economics assignment involves students in just such a process of policy-making.

The Industries Assistance Commission believes that continuation or extension of the present structure of assistance will inhibit Australia's economic growth in the future. (I.A.C. Annual Report 1974–5). Present a reasoned argument to support or refute the Commission's belief.

It is your invitation to compile a battery of reasons for or against the existing system of protective tariffs and subsidies and tax concessions for industry. Your argument would be built up on a variety of data relating to the current fortunes of individual industries and how they correlate with the general levels of prosperity, and would also examine common economic assumptions about the capacity of natural market forces to promote economic growth in Australia.

Argumentative writing is often stimulated by the need to investigate the assumption or assumptions that underlie a particular proposition. Those assumptions may be taken for granted as valid grounds or warrants for the argument, but their validity is not unchallengeable and they themselves raise other, broader questions. Exercises of this kind are quite common in philosophy, but also in the social sciences, where ethical and social issues are concerned. A proposition may be offered as a stimulus, for instance:

Women who stay at home should be paid as part of the work force. Discuss.

You might recognize this as a challenge to the assumption that only men automatically become part of the paid work force and become entitled to receive an income either from their employer or in the form of unemployment relief from the government. This assumption raises a host of other issues, including:

- What is work?
- Are all adults entitled to an income?
- Is work at home "work"?
- How can domestic work be costed?
- Who would pay for it?

- Should men be entitled to receive such pay?

These further issues will supply topics for discussion and generate the argumentative grounds for your answer.

In controversial areas such as this, there is no right or wrong response, just better and less well argued cases. But the more satisfying argumentative writing takes account of the arguments on both sides as far as possible, and you might begin by compiling the two sets, rather as if you were weighing them on a balance. The case for paying women who choose to stay at home rests largely on egalitarian principles, whereas the case against rests on the economic difficulties it would cause. In your answer you would probably throw your weight into the scales one way or the other. But your commitment to one or the other will be the more impressive if, as already suggested, you show a responsiveness to the issues on both sides.

Writers may choose to present their cases according to one of two possible strategies, aiming either for (a) maximum impact, or (b) optimum acceptability for the argument – if you like, either power or solidarity. The older tradition of persuasion, stretching back ultimately to the oratory of Greece and Rome, was to aim for powerful impact and to discredit opposing views. Such tactics were moulded by their use in legal proceedings, when a client's life or reputation might be at stake. The appropriateness of that practice for academic argumentation has been questioned,[5] and some advocate a different tactic based on the principle of seeking all possible bases for agreement with the reader. This is often called "Rogerian" argument, after the psychotherapist Carl Rogers. It derives from his experience of the interview situation and the need to avoid putting the other person on the defensive – again not exactly the academic writing situation. Nevertheless in the hands of a careful writer it can be a remarkably effective method of persuasion, a means of letting the other person have your way!

Your choice of one or other strategy will affect the structure of your argumentation. To maximize the impact of your case, you would set the most powerful arguments at the beginning and end of the essay and grasp every opportunity to knock out opposing arguments along the way. An impact-oriented version of the case against women who stay at home becoming part of the paid work force would stress the enormous expense and the difficulty of putting dollar values on domestic work. It might incidentally try to undermine the suggestion that this was "work" in any accepted sense of the word.

The much more conciliatory Rogerian approach would probably begin with an issue that is problematical whichever side you take: What is work? If it is defined either in terms of "duties performed" or "duties performed outside the home", it becomes difficult to argue for the right of the unemployed to an income, and this undermines any general assumptions about an adult's right to be paid. The problems of defining "work" link up with more specific questions about the nature and cost-value of what women do at home. Women's very versatility compounds the problem. Thus a case against paying women at home can be made without resorting to heavy-handed rhetorical tactics.

Of course your choice of argumentative style may be restricted by the set topic or the arguments at your disposal. But it is a good idea to consider alternative argumentative tactics in order to find the best way of representing your case. As you consider, you might also take into account the attitudes of the departmental staff for whom you are writing – whether they are varied, or relatively monolithic, and whether they are likely to be receptive or unreceptive to your case. In academic contexts, the impact-oriented approach is effective when readers share your views but tends to raise hackles if they don't. (It probably has wider power to impress in ordinary public communication.)

NOTES
1. The certainty of scientific or any other knowledge is of course a matter of philosophical debate.
2. Interpretations may also revolve around a single word, as in the question: Did the governor-general act *constitutionally* when he withdrew Mr Whitlam's commission as prime minister?
3. Marxist, Freudian and other classic interpretations of a well-known piece of children's literature are humorously presented in *The Pooh Perplex* (Dutton, New York, 1963) by Frederick Crews.
4. Some evaluative writing centres on words with sharper connotations, for example, *How precise was Homer's knowledge of the geography of the Aegean*

area? Yet their value is still relative to context. Geographical precision in poetry and in cartography are obviously different, and a relevant criterion of precision would have to be formulated.

5. See R. E. Young, A. L. Becker, and K. L. Pike, *Rhetoric: Discovery and Change* (Harcourt, Brace, World, New York, 1970).

5
Information at a glance

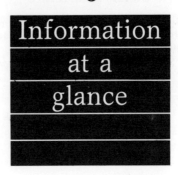

Readers as a breed are an impatient lot. They are usually looking for quick returns on their investment of time and welcome any opportunity to gain information in summary form. Though academic writing is a discursive business in principle, there are several accepted means of supplying summarized information to the reader, both the **non-verbal** summaries of tables, graphs and diagrams, and the **verbal** ones of introductions and conclusions. Each has a conventional location in a piece of writing: the verbal summaries at either the beginning or end, and the non-verbal ones in the middle (unless they cover many pages, in which case they are often set in an appendix).

These two forms of summary are not equally acceptable in all disciplines, however. Non-verbal summaries are not usually welcome in the older disciplines (for a discussion of the antiquity of academic disciplines, see chapter 1) and so tables and diagrams are to be avoided when writing in the humanities (for example in literature, history and philosophy) and also in law. There the writer must rely on words alone.

But non-verbal summaries come into their own in the sciences, and there writers are expected to report experimental data in the form of tables and graphs, and to provide diagrams and figures to show the shapes and proportions of any complex physical things under discussion. The presentations would be extremely cumbersome without them. In the social sciences, too, tables and graphs and maps are often used along the way to help present the quantitative or distributional information on which an argument is based. The full range of summary devices can be exploited by writers in the "younger" disciplines.

Although introductions and conclusions are common to writing in all disciplines, their use in a report is somewhat different from their use in an essay. In a report both are formally separated and identified by means of headings, and their contents are differently linked with the body of the report. We shall therefore reserve discussion of report introductions and conclusions until the next chapter and concentrate here on the introductions and conclusions of essays. They will be the subject of the first section of this chapter, followed by the various non-verbal aids to communication.

Essay introductions and conclusions

Everyone knows that an essay isn't an essay without an introduction and a conclusion! They are an accepted and expected part of essay-writing convention, used to frame the main body of the essay. They give it a certain rough symmetry. But their actual form and content is a hazy matter for many, and we should spend a little time discussing them. The writing of introductions and conclusions is in fact a relatively straightforward matter once the body of the essay has been thought out, and this is why we have delayed talking about them until after chapters 3 and 4.

The functions of introductions and conclusions are of course to forecast what the reader is about to receive, and to consolidate the thrust of the essay at its end. Both involve some type of overview of the body of the essay. But their perspectives are, or should be, different because of their locations at opposite ends of the essay, and it is a pity to use the same kind of summary statement in both places. Few readers appreciate being first told what is to come, then being told it, and then being told what they've been told! It gives the impression of zero development within the essay. The discussion should take the reader somewhere, and a repetitious conclusion suggests that it hasn't left home base. Both introduction and conclusion should anticipate the reader's angle on what is communicated in the body of the essay. His/her **prospective** needs are to be catered for in the introduction, and **retrospective** needs in the conclusion.

At the start the reader needs to know the subject and scope of the essay as well as why it is of interest. Yet those needs can be met in many ways other than by beginning with the words of the question or topic set in a carrier phrase: "This essay is concerned with how . . ." or "This essay tackles the question of whether . . .". (These, alas, are the dull beginnings of many a dull essay.) You must of course indicate which question you are applying yourself to, but this can be done by means of a heading. The opening paragraph can then be used to stimulate the reader's interest and appetite for what is to come.

Professional writers often begin with a striking quotation or a brief but graphic illustration to highlight the issue(s) to be discussed. Looking for a provocative opener to an essay on recent Soviet–U.S. relations, we could, for example, make use of Khrushchev's enigmatic statement: "We will bury you." Let us suppose the essay is to discuss the question "Did the character of Soviet–U.S. relations change after the death of Stalin?" Its introduction might run as follows:

"Khrushchev's remark 'We will bury you', uttered in a meeting with Western diplomats in Moscow in 1957, struck fear into the hearts of many Americans. By others it was shrugged off as communist rhetoric, as perhaps a mistranslation of the chorus of the revolutionary hymn: 'We shall overcome'. In retrospect, its message remains ambiguous: possibly the ultimate threat, or possibly a futuristic claim that 'Our society will outlast yours'. Ambiguity and ambivalence were certainly the characteristics of Soviet–U.S. relations during Khrushchev's regime (the period on which this essay will concentrate) and that, if nothing else, represented a change from the Cold War days of Stalin . . ."

Controversial statements and dramatic illustrations are not the only way to begin an essay, but they do grab the reader's attention and stimulate interest in the pages to follow (to your advantage, when your essay may, after all, be thirty-ninth in the pile!). The chief danger with such introductions, or any introduction, is that it may seem to open up the subject too widely for any writer to handle within the word limit. If the introduction seems to promise things that are not discussed later in the essay, it will leave the reader dissatisfied and with the feeling that it hasn't delivered the goods. Avoiding this is mostly a matter of using the introduction to mould the reader's expectations and bring them into line with what the essay can and will deliver.

An introductory quotation, like all quotations, calls for a follow-up comment from the writer to show how it is being interpreted and used. You can use this follow-up comment to define the subject of your essay, as in the sample introduction above. Note how it also indicates the limits of the essay's coverage (only Khrushchev's years, not the later sixties or seventies), so as to avoid disappointing the reader later on. The follow-up comment can also introduce the essay's general proposition (see chapter 2, pages 19 to 22), which here is to the effect that there has been continual shifting in Soviet–U.S. relations since Stalin. As in this case, the propositional statement is ideally specific enough to provide direction for the essay, but not so specific as to pre-empt the later discussion. It is a pity to give away the details of your conclusion at the start.

In an ordinary essay of one to two thousand words, the introduction may occupy one or two paragraphs, depending on the length of the opening gambit and how much has to be said by way of follow-up. Apart from indicating the scope and theme of the essay with it, you may want to comment on the kinds of evidence or source material to be used. Again, it will help to prevent a reader saying, "But you forgot or didn't take into account x and y," if you say at the start that you only intend to look at w and z. All these preliminaries will certainly fill the opening paragraph(s), but they should not be allowed to take you into any particular points of the discussion.

The general and strategic statements of the introduction give way to the "action" of the body of the essay, and this is usually marked by increasing density of detail as the writer grapples with individual issues. This change from the more general to the more particular is the usual sign to readers that they are now in the main body of the discussion. There is thus no need to signpost the introduction and body with headings, and by convention they are absent from essays.

There is no formal signposting of the conclusion in an essay either, and this is obviously a worry to many essay-writers, who make a habit of prefacing the final paragraph with the phrase "In conclusion". The anxious labelling of that paragraph suggests a surprising lack of confidence in the simple fact that the conclusion is always visibly close to the end. The deeper worry, no doubt, is how to distil a conclusion out of the preceding discussion, and the conclusiveness of the ending will depend on what has or has not been achieved in the body. But let us assume that a number of points have been effectively discussed in the body and there is substance on which to conclude.

The conclusion interacts with the dominant character of the body of the essay, and its contents will vary depending on the kind of discussion you have provided. We might distinguish five types of conclusion, corresponding to the five types of writing discussed in chapters 3 and 4.

	BODY	CONCLUSION
expository *pages 26 to 34*	data presented in schematized form	reviews main units of discussion
explanatory *pages 35 to 38*	interrelationships in data discussed	highlights explanatory principle used
interpretive *pages 41 to 45*	data examined in terms of key/model	asserts viability of interpretation
evaluative *pages 45 to 48*	criteria applied systematically to data	formulates value judgment
argumentative *pages 48 to 52*	grounds and warrants of argument discussed	affirms validity of argument

TABLE 2: Conclusions to different kinds of discussion

In general terms the conclusion is there to express the collective significance of all the material you have presented. It should show what it all adds up to. It requires you to step back for a broader view, after all the detailed discussion, to take the view "from the ridges", and to make more general statements about it. In an interpretive essay like the one on Soviet-U.S. relations introduced a page or two ago, you would be presenting your material with a particular interpretation in mind, namely the continual changes and adjustments to policy. To show this you would have described the events of the fifties and early sixties and detailed some in which Soviet actions, from the U.S. point of view, seemed aggressive, and others in which a desire for rapprochement could be seen (for example, the Berlin ultimatum, and its postponement; the installation of missiles in Cuba, and their withdrawal). The themes of aggression and rapprochement would have been expressed from time to time in the course of the discussion, but they can be asserted with much more conviction as you conclude. By that stage they are vindicated by all the preceding data and will emerge as valid generalizations about it.

Apart from using the conclusion to underscore your themes or generalizations, the conclusion is the place to link them up with the central proposition made through the essay, and so reinforce *it*. In our sample essay, the introductory proposition concerned the ambivalence of Soviet foreign policy after Stalin (see page 56), and it would be amply supported by the proposed generalizations about threats as well as concessions, particularly if you stressed the alternation between them. The conclusions would thus **synthesize**, or weave together, the various strands of the discussion.

So far we have emphasized the retrospective role of the generalizations in the conclusion. But they may also provide the base for one final advance in the essay, for example in a final judgment. Again, this must interact with what has gone before (no new material should be brought into the conclusion), but it can embody a widened perspective on the familiar material and a stimulating close for the essay. Our sample essay could very well conclude its interpretive description of Soviet–U.S. relations by weighing up the relative importance of *aggression* and *desire for rapprochement* in the overall pattern of ambivalence. A final judgment could then be formulated as to whether Soviet–U.S. relations were on balance better or worse by the end of Khrushchev's regime. Such a judgment would epitomize the longer-term significance of the Khrushchev years and invite the reader to relate them to the ongoing forces of twentieth-century history.

A closing move that widens perspectives like this helps to stimulate the reader as you take your leave. It is one of the most reliable ways of creating a final impact, though not the only one. Some writers, notably editorial writers, like to end with a flamboyant phrase or sentence, and this is not a bad idea, provided its point is congruous with the rest of the conclusion. A quirky or tangential afterthought will only detract from the discussion, and it is more important to ensure the intellectual impact of your conclusion. One way or another it should consolidate the discussion and come as the culmination of what you and your reader have been through over several pages! A neat summary of your themes, a synthesis of your generalizations and the original proposition, or a final judgment – any of these can be an effective reminder of what your essay has achieved.

NON-VERBAL SUMMARY DEVICES

Both conclusions and introductions differ from other kinds of summaries by being much more strategic. With them you mould the reader's initial and ultimate view of the whole essay, and though they project and reflect its contents, they do not simply summarize them.

The summary devices about to be considered – tables, graphs, diagrams, drawings, maps – are very much content-centred. They present limited blocks of information in the body of an essay and have no particular responsibility as far as the whole is concerned. They most often represent numerical information or physical shape and proportions, although both tables and diagrams can be used to display a set of more abstract relationships. (See, for example, the tables on pages 58 and

92–93, and the diagrams on pages 87 and 113.) Diagrams are also used to express dynamic relationships, for example the sequence of events in a regular process, or a sequence of options, as in computer diagrams. Such diagrams are also called **flow-charts**.

Tables have the virtue of condensing a lot of statistical information into a small space and ordering it so as to permit both horizontal and vertical comparisons. The following table presenting the incomes earned by men and women of Sydney in several categories is informative in this respect:

INCOME GROUP	MEN	WOMEN
Over $26 000	61 000	6 000
$18 000 to 26 000	136 000	23 000
$12 000 to 18 000	317 000	116 000
$8000 to 12 000	258 000	199 000
$4000 to 8000	143 000	234 000
$2000 to 4000	134 000	256 000
Less than $2000	24 000	100 000
Zero	70 000	242 000

TABLE 3: *Showing the relative incomes of men and women over fifteen years of age in Sydney, N.S.W. (Figures taken from the 1981 census)*

Some interesting contrasts emerge from a table such as this. It shows up the fact that the majority of male incomes are between $8000 and $18 000, while the largest groups of female incomes are less than $8000. The relative scarcity of female incomes above $18 000 is also evident.

But the two sets of figures in table 3 cannot be compared very exactly across income groups, because the total populations of males and females surveyed here were different (a total of 1 143 000 and 1 176 000 females). For proper comparison, both sets of raw figures need to be expressed in terms of percentages, as shown in table 4.

With these percentages, proper horizontal comparisons can be made, and they make clear the different representation of the two sexes in each income group.

INCOME GROUP	MEN	WOMEN
Over $26 000	5.0%	0.5%
$18 000 to 26 000	12.0%	2.0%
$12 000 to 18 000	28.0%	10.0%
$8000 to 12 000	23.0%	17.0%
$4000 to 8000	12.0%	20.0%
$2000 to 4000	12.0%	22.0%
Less than $2000	2.0%	8.5%
Zero	6.0%	20.0%

TABLE 4: Showing the percentages of Sydney males and females in eight income groups (based on the raw figures of table 3)

The overall patterns in sets of figures can be effectively presented by means of graphs. When plotted on a graph, the shape of the resultant curve or the angles of the line show the relative evenness or unevenness of the distribution. If you draw a graph of the percentage figures of table 4, the resulting "curves" are both skewed, that is, not symmetrical, but displaced to the right or left of centre. This shows that the data is not distributed "normally" (in terms of a normal curve).[1] (See figure 8, page 63.)

The two scales of a graph normally start from zero, as shown in figure 8. The numbers are written upright, but the labelling is done parallel to the axis. The two axes need to be fully and clearly labelled so that a reader can "read" the graph without reference to the accompanying prose. The steps on a graph are normally scaled continuously, that is, they are all the same size, so it would be important to indicate here that this is *not* the case on the horizontal axis (the steps are smaller nearer to zero and get progessively bigger). Because this is so, our graphs are somewhat compacted in shape. The male/female difference in the upper income brackets would appear even more marked if the same-sized steps were used all the way across.[2] Even so, the graph effectively shows up the different distributions of men's and women's incomes, and facilitates overall comparisons of the two sets of figures.

Certain standard forms of diagram offer us still other ways

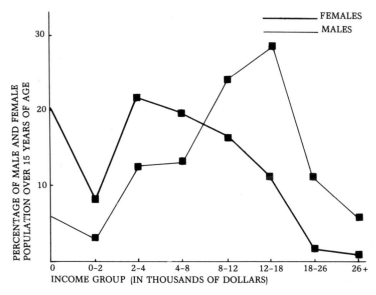

FIGURE 8: *Graph showing the percentages of Sydney male and female incomes in eight income groups*

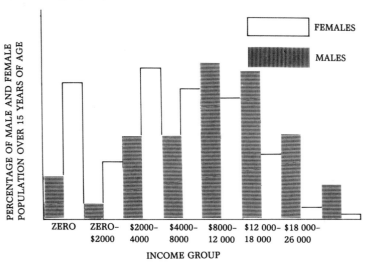

FIGURE 9: *Bar diagram showing the numbers of Sydney male and female incomes in each of eight income groups*

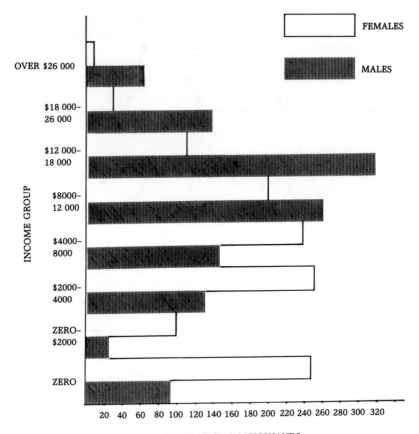

FIGURE 10: Histogram showing the percentages of Sydney male and female incomes in each of eight income groups

of representing and comparing statistics. They are (a) the histogram, (b) the bar diagram, and (c) the pie diagram.

(a) HISTOGRAM
The histogram is really a bar diagram turned round ninety degrees. The relative heights of the rectangles now provide the comparative information, this time in terms of percentages (that is, those of table 4). Had we used the raw figures, the diagram

would have been a little more difficult to read than the equivalent bar diagram because of the lack of parallel vertical lines against which to size up the long rectangles.

(b) BAR DIAGRAM
In this we are again using the raw frequencies of table 3, and the relative lengths of the bars make for easy visual comparison of the numbers in each income group.

(c) PIE DIAGRAM

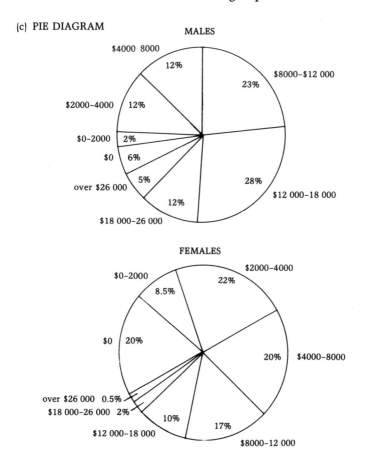

FIGURE 11: *Pie diagrams showing the percentage division of the male and female population of Sydney among eight income groups*

Pie diagrams are normally devised on a percentage basis, so we have put our percentage figures to use again here. These diagrams are less effective for expressing comparisons, because each set of values needs a separate diagram. There is no way of superimposing a second set of values on the same diagram.

These various forms of non-verbal summary are clearly not all equally useful for communicating the same kind of information. It is, as always, a case of choosing the one most suitable for the task and considering what you want to demonstrate and how many comparisons you want to make at once. Multiple comparisons are most easily shown on graphs.

DRAWINGS

For communicating certain kinds of physical information, drawings are indispensable. Only with the aid of a drawing can you really convey the proportions and details of the size and shape of a composite object, or the layout of interconnected objects. It would be impossible to explain the structure of most biological organisms without recourse to drawing, and sketches have an important part to play in expository and explanatory writing in the natural sciences. The following drawing represents

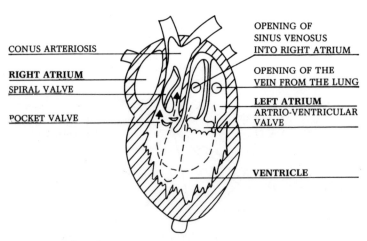

FIGURE 12: A frog's heart (ventral view)

the structure of a frog's heart more accurately and concisely than could be done by words alone.

Drawings like this must be done to scale so that the various components are in correct proportion to each other. They can show only two dimensions satisfactorily, and so it is important to indicate which perspective on the object is being offered, where this is not self-evident. The note above, "ventral view" (as opposed to dorsal view), is there for this reason. The number of labels on the drawing should coincide with the number of terms introduced in the surrounding commentary.

MAPS

In order to discuss the geographical distribution of some natural or social phenomenon, you may need to introduce a map as an aid in your writing. It is your prime aid for communicating locational and distributional information, whether it is the active volcanoes of the world or the migration of the mutton bird, the spread of Creole languages or the concentrations of rented dwellings in Sydney.

A map like this gives full visual support to any comment you might want to make about the evenness or unevenness of a

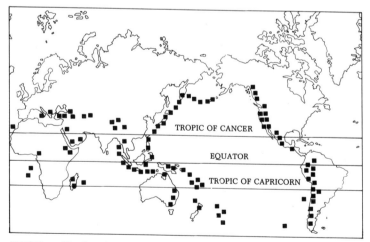

FIGURE 13: The locations of geologically recent volcanoes

distribution. (The concentration of volcanoes along the Pacific coasts is one thing that emerges very clearly from this map.) Like drawings, maps need to be drawn to scale, though it is accepted that sketch maps in exams are likely to be rough and that a quick map of South America, for instance, is likely to resemble a carrot.

All the communicative aids mentioned in this chapter help the reader as well as the writer. They offer the reader a neat overview of parts of your material and, in the case of introductions and conclusions, a perspective (either prospective or retrospective) over the whole. By giving readers better access to your material, you help them to appreciate better what you are offering, and the advantage from then on is all yours.

NOTES

1. This and other useful statistical notions are fully described in any elementary book on statistics, such as *A Basic Course in Statistics, with Sociological Applications*, T. R Anderson and M. Zelditch (Holt, Rinehart, Winston, New York, 1968).
2. The various ways of representing and misrepresenting statistical facts are amusingly and informatively discussed by Darrell Huff, in *How to Lie with Statistics* (Norton, New York, 1954).

6

Reports

Introduction

Method, Results

Discussion/Conclusion

Abstracts

Reports are a favourite means of communicating in many institutions apart from universities and colleges. In the public service, in hospitals, in industry and elsewhere, reports are written about places and patients and problems, and the size and contents of the report can be varied to suit the task. They may be as brief as a single page or as long as a royal commission. They are both formal and flexible vehicles for information.

But students are never invited to vary the shape of their reports. Their reports must conform to a standard pattern, one established in the science disciplines and used there and elsewhere (for example, in psychology or acoustic phonetics) to present experimental findings. The standard report format consists of four or five sections (introduction, method, results, discussion and/or conclusion) that are always presented in a fixed order.

Yet, however conventional this format, it is not arbitrary. It confronts us with the empirical nature of all scientific data and reminds us that experimental findings and conclusions must always be seen in terms of how they are reached. The format obliges you to show in full detail how you obtained your results and allows others to check and duplicate them if they wish. This is why so much space is given to the procedures followed in the experiment; and also why the experimental results are kept separate from your interpretation of them, so that others can review them independently and perhaps consider alternative conclusions. This, as one scientist puts it, is where science begins.[1] So the format of scientific reports represents some of the most fundamental principles of scientific inquiry.

Writing reports may not be a student's favourite activity, but the effort of using the format regularly and presenting your work in its terms helps to make empirical practices thoroughly familiar. The format also has the advantage of freeing you from the writer's usual obligation to find a suitable structure for the raw material, which was our concern in chapters 3 and 4. Essay writing places this responsibility very much on the individual, and a structure needs to be devised to suit both the material and the particular purpose (whether explanatory, evaluative, etc.) of the exercise. Report writers, meanwhile, work within a prefabricated structure.

Students in science courses are normally given some advice on the setting out of experimental reports through the laboratory or departmental manual. It will indicate the presentation practices you are expected to adopt, as well as local technical conventions. It may have something to say about style, such as keeping your expression concise and impersonal. (These things are discussed with other stylistic matters in chapters 7 and 8.) Yet it may have little to say about the communicative function of each of the sections of the standard report. In fact surprisingly little is written about these functions, as if they were self-evident from the headings themselves. A quick comparison of the functions of an essay introduction (pages 55 to 57) and a report introduction (to follow) shows quite a big difference in what goes in under that heading.

The sections of a report have essential individual functions, but are also interdependent. The longer the report, the more planning this requires. We shall take the rest of this chapter to look over both individual and collective roles of the introduction, method, results, discussion and conclusion, and, finally, the preparation of abstracts.

INTRODUCTION

In the introduction to an experimental report, your aim and purpose in conducting the experiment are the essential things to communicate. In a brief report they will be one and the same, and may be just titled "Aim". The following statements might be all that is used to introduce experiments in chemistry:

(a) *To determine the amount of carbonate present in a commercial waste product*
(b) *To prepare and standardize a solution of potassium permanganate*

As these two show, many experiments done by students are concerned with either making a chemical product or analysing and measuring the components of given compounds. Where alternative methods exist (for example, measuring by gravimetric or volumetric analysis), the one used might be indicated in this first statement about the experiment.

The statement will be a plain one. There are no prizes for striking introductions in report writing, and to express the aim of a botanical experiment as *"How much salt can a dicotyledon take?"* is likely to do more harm than good. Precision is much more important than originality of expression. In your lab work you are normally re-enacting a standard experiment, or else making use of established principles and methods for analytical purposes. Your awareness of this and familiarity with the facts are best communicated by repeating the standard forms of expression.

But in longer reports the introduction does more than simply express the aim, and there is room and need for more individual writing. The specific aim of the experiment may well crystallize a wider exploratory purpose, and both need to be introduced. The exploration will probably be linked with one or more hypotheses, and much experimental work in psychology, for instance, involves the testing of hypotheses. The hypotheses will need to be set out accompanied by relevant theoretical issues or historical background, to provide a well-defined context for the experiment. The type of background material will relate to the focus of the experiment and will vary according to whether it is primarily method- or theory-oriented.

In a **hypothesis-testing** experiment it is important to document the current state of the hypothesis. So, with the following experiment in the area of social psychology:

The experiment tests the hypothesis that differential judgments are made by Australians about those whom they hear using the Broad accent, and the Educated or Cultivated accent,

the writer would need to present the findings of any research already conducted on this. If none has been done in this country, studies from other parts of the English-speaking world might be introduced. The relevance of overseas studies to the Australian scene would also be worth commenting on. The background information could be presented in chronological order, which would help to show how the current hypothesis evolved. Alternatively, if scholarly opinion diverges significantly, the presentation could be units representing different schools of thought.

When the experiment is prompted by problems in the **methodology** of earlier ones, the introductory survey would categorize earlier work in terms of the methods and procedures used. Were you, for example, concerned that judgments about accents might be affected by the perceived authenticity of the speech samples used, you might want to compare the results of experiments that used the "matched guise"[2] with those using the non-"matched guise" technique. Your survey would then highlight this aspect of earlier experiments. It might contain a somewhat different selection of previous experiments from those used to introduce the hypothesis-testing experiment.

The background or "literature" survey of the introduction not only creates a context for your experiment, but also indicates your purpose in broader discipline terms. It needs to be kept within bounds, however, and should not bulk so large that it dwarfs the rest of your report. Instead of trying to cover every previous experiment in the field, your survey should select those with findings that are either challenged or confirmed by your own work. You may in fact want to say how your work shapes up in relation to them and to foreshadow in general terms the results of your experiment, for instance:

(a) *The results of this experiment support/refute the current hypothesis;*

or

(b) *The consistency of results obtained in this experiment suggests that the method used here is a more reliable way of analysing/ measuring the variable than those used in previous studies of this kind.*

Statements like these help to provide the reader with an appropriate mental set for the details of the experiment, without giving away too much too early. Foreshadowing statements are of course not needed if an abstract is placed at the beginning of the report, as required by some departments (and most journals). (Abstracts are discussed on pages 80 to 81.)

METHOD

The method section of a report should present all the details of the experiment that need to be known by anyone who wants to replicate it. When reporting routine experiments, the details can be simply described in operational order, but in more extensive and exploratory work the method section may be divided into two, or three or four subsections, including materials, apparatus, procedures and subjects.

To take the simplest case first: a classic procedure for making or measuring a chemical product is usually reported step by step, with all the details on materials and procedures in together, for example:

A measure of 1 g of acetanilide was dissolved in 5 mL of glacial acetic acid in a 100 mL conical flask. 0.6 g of sodium bromide and 0.5 g of sodium bromate were added, and the mixture was then gently heated over a micro-burner and given a careful shake from time to time. The procedure was continued until the solution became a permanent bromine colour . . .

Information is offered in a straightforward way, much like a narrative. But the style is very unlike that of a narrative and deliberately avoids all reference to the human agent of the actions. (This impersonal style and the tendency to use passive rather than active expression are discussed on pages 108 and 109.)

But the information in the method section of a longer report is differently arranged and presented. The actual procedures are described separately from the materials and apparatus, and all are covered in great detail. It is always better to give too much rather than too little information to ensure replicability. For example, under Materials it might be important to detail some aspects of the chemical compounds you used, such as their purity and structure, as well as the source of the material and the method of preparation, if relevant. Chemical or pharmacological compounds can be named according to local convention, although if using a trade name you should give the chemical formulation beside it on first mention, for example:

Condy's crystals (that is, potassium permanganate).

Items of apparatus can also be referred to in trade terms, and for the most exact specification both the brand and the model of equipment should be mentioned, for example:

Beyer type DT 96 headphones with circumaural cushions.

You should nevertheless be able to specify the equipment used in *non*-trade terms, that is, know the principles by which it operates, because they may affect the experimental findings. When several pieces of equipment have been used, it is helpful to list them, with exact sizes and dimensions. Sometimes the layout of equipment is unusual and calls for comment. If apparatus has been specially constructed for the experiment, the most reliable way of documenting it is by diagrams, which are usually clearer than a thousand words for such purposes. In psychology and education experiments, the format and appearance of stimulus materials are important and need to be described under "Apparatus" or photocopied for inclusion in the appendix.

With the materials and/or apparatus described in full, the account of procedures follows as a separate section, and they, too, need to be covered in detail. In a psychology experiment the instructions given to the subjects can influence their responses and the experimental results, so every instruction must be carefully documented. Normally you would relate the procedures in operational order, as with the chemistry example presented on the previous page, though if the experiment involved a series of tests and trials these can be most effectively explained by means of a table. In the example that follows, the table shows two measures of the solubility of a chemical[3] at different temperatures.

TEMP. °C	SOLUBILITY p.p.m.	SOLUBILITY mol/kg
100	658	0.00890
120	433	0.00585
140	277	0.00374
160	185	0.00250
180	129	0.00174
200	99	0.00134

TABLE 5: *The solubility of calcium hydroxide at different temperatures*

The non-verbal presentation clarifies such a sequence of operations. The rationale for the series of tests might be explained as a follow-up to the table.

In more advanced experimental work you might have decided to use some particular statistical technique for interpreting the results, and this would need to be justified in your procedures section.[4] But this is not likely to be necessary in earlier years, when the statistical techniques are prescribed for you.

The selection of subjects for the experiment is also an important aspect of much work in biology and animal sciences, as well as in medicine and psychology. The characteristics of the subjects are usually given a separate section, usually at the start of the method section. (We have delayed discussing them only because they do not need to be mentioned in reports in all kinds of science courses.) Apart from the actual numbers of subjects, all relevant aspects of their identity need to be reported. In biology or veterinary science, you should say what type of animals were used and comment on their genetic background, age, sex and size. For instance:

A total of 20 Lincoln cross-bred ewes were used in the experiment. They were two-year-olds averaging 50 kg.

In the human sciences, the subjects' psycho-social characteristics may be as important as physical ones, and a wide range of other factors may need to be mentioned, such as intelligence and level of education, ethnic background, and social and family status:

The forty subjects were first-year psychology students at Macquarie University, twenty males and twenty females, ranging in age from eighteen to twenty-five years. All were Australian-born and unmarried at the time of the experiment . . .

Some of the characteristics reported would be crucial to the experiment itself (as "unmarried" would be in a study of current attitudes to marriage); others are there to standardize the population studied so as to avoid irregularities among the experimental results, caused by a hotch-potch of subject variables. (The details on age, ethnicity and level of education might be of this kind in our hypothetical study on attitudes to marriage.)

The experimenter may use both an experimental and a "control" group and would, of course, report any intrinsic differences between them. But often enough the experimental and control groups form a homogeneous population; it is just that they are differently treated in the experiment, and those differences would be described under Procedures. Either way, the use of a control group would be recorded among the details of the method and would allow you, in the later discussion, to highlight any differences between its pattern of responses and that of the experimental group.

RESULTS

The results section of a report is used to present the data produced by the experiment and to describe briefly any trends that appear in them. This is the place to draw attention to both regularities and any anomalies in the data, though your interpretation of them, and any theoretical explanation of them, should be reversed for the discussion section.

In principle, experimental data must be reported so that anyone who wished could check or rework the findings. However, when the raw data bulks large and provides little ready information for the reader, it is commonly set in an appendix. The results section then contains only data that has been predigested, that is, processed according to any established statistical procedure (means and standard deviations, statistical tests of significance, percentages, etc.).

Much of the results section consists of data summaries in graphic form. The trends in your data can be shown both accurately and effectively by means of the various tables and diagrams discussed in the previous chapter (pages 60 to 66). Your choice among them would depend on whether you are dealing with raw or processed data, what internal contrasts you wanted to highlight, and what comparisons you wanted to make. Tables, bar diagrams and histograms show up internal differences in the data, while graphs make more conspicuous the overall patterns and trends. As noted in the previous chapter, your graphs and tables need clear labels to explain the kinds of values they embody. An explanatory title is helpful to the reader, and there is no harm in having it run to more than one line. When offering several graphs and tables, it helps if you indicate which part of the experiment each relates to.

The order in which you present your data summaries is very much in your hands. There is no need to follow the operational order of the experiment; it is better to seek a logical sequence, for example, beginning with the findings on the more general or fundamental variable, and then proceeding to more specialized ones (cf. pages 30 to 31).

Though graphs and tables are usually the staple of your results section, each one requires a brief follow-up comment. The trend shown in a graph may seem unmistakable to you, but you should describe it in words, too, to underscore it and ensure it doesn't escape the reader. If the data summary shows no very remarkable trends, this, too, should be verbally acknowledged, for negative findings can be as important as positive ones when experimenting. The observations that you make in the results section must be strictly empirical, but they form the bridge between the specifics of the experiment and your ultimate conclusions.

It almost goes without saying that the words *significant* and *significance* should not be used in talking about your results unless they link up with statistical tests of significance. If they do, you would, of course, record the levels of probability, presenting them in a table and again drawing attention to them in an accompanying comment. You will certainly want to appeal to them in later discussion.

DISCUSSION/CONCLUSION

The latter section or sections of a report are used to articulate the value of the experiment and to explore the experimental findings. The extensiveness of the discussion depends very much on the scope of the experiment and whether it is routine laboratory work or more extensive and exploratory. If it is in the first category, it will require only a short report with just a conclusion following the results section (see (a) below); if in the second it will be longer, and some discussion is expected from you before you state your conclusion(s), (see (b), below). Let us look at each of these in turn.

(a) In short reports where you are simply writing up standard experiments, there is little to discuss and a conclusion is all that is needed. In it you would simply review your own results in the light of the original aim of the experiment. If by good management you achieved the intended product or result, you will mostly be affirming that the particular method works. If the experiment had you making physical or chemical measurements, you would need to say whether they were in line with what might be predicted from the scientific principles involved. Such conclusions are still not very elaborate. You simply draw attention to the compatibility of your results with the particular scientific principle(s), wording your statements in terms that can usually be derived from the laboratory manual or textbook.

When there are discrepancies between your reports and those that would be predicted from the principles involved, you should offer some sort of explanation as to why. Is there any pattern in the discrepancies that suggests regular interference from an identifiable factor? The search for such an explanation will make constructive use of non-conforming results, and writing about them naturally makes the conclusion a little longer. Curiously, there is less to say after a successful experiment than after a not-so-successful one.

(b) In longer reports the conclusion(s) cannot be related to the textbook, and they are very much dependent on your discussion and interpretation of the results. The conclusion therefore has to follow the discussion, which is often a longish and quite wide-ranging section. It is nevertheless kept within bounds by the terms of the introduction, and its central function is to relate the experimental results to the original aim and purpose. The key question to explore is whether the results help to satisfy the stated aim and whether they confirm or refute any associated hypothesis.

Sometimes the results are very clear cut, and in the discussion you have only to underscore the observations made in your results section and show how they provide an answer to the issues raised in the introduction. The trends represented in your numerical findings, and their statistical significance, may settle any doubts about the basic hypothesis or else suggest that it is misconceived. Either way, the discussion need not be elaborate; it just has to point the reader on to the straightforward conclusion.

More often the implications of the results have to be teased out and chewed over, in relation to both the experimental and the theoretical context. In the discussion you would try to link the statistical findings with details of the experimental conditions. Here you would highlight subject variables and any contrasts between the experimental and control-group results, as well as any inconsistent results that may have been caused by the form of the experiment. Experiments always have their limits, and it shows critical thinking to point out the extent to which your results are valid and the domains into which they should not be extrapolated.

If your experiment was conducted along much the same lines as some earlier ones, you would want to make comparisons with them. Ideally they would already have been outlined in the introduction, so it would simply be a case of minimal reference here, reminding the reader of them and not taking time off to present them from scratch. The discussion is meant as a vehicle for exploring *your* findings, not a further survey of other people's.

Your other task is to link your findings with the broader theoretical issues implied or explicitly introduced in the introduction. You may have presented the experiment as a means of testing aspects of a given theoretical model and would now comment on the correlation between your actual findings and the theoretical expectations. Are they in agreement, or at odds? Could the findings be explained as well (or better) by another theory? You will in fact be engaged in an interpretive exercise like those discussed in an earlier chapter (pages 40 to 44), and be using one or more theoretical models as an interpretive key to your data.

As you pursue this discussion you will be formulating some conclusions, and possibly further questions. Ideas for future research often suggest themselves, and it is worthwhile noting them, though not digressing on to them. As one scientist has put it: "Once round the hypothesis-tests circuit is usually as much as the experiment and the data will stand."[5] Both conclusions and questions will emerge along the way in your discussion, and are important products of it. To prevent them being buried, it is a good idea to repeat them as a group at the close of the report. The questions for future research are, of course, open-ended and would make inconclusive material on which to finish, so they are normally grouped together just before the final paragraph.

The final paragraph, often set apart with its own heading, is then reserved for your conclusions. They can be presented as a summary paragraph or in point form, depending on how coherent a set they form. Either way they should be succinct – they have the backing of the whole report to justify them!

ABSTRACTS

Though abstracts are commonly placed at the beginning of a report, they can really only be written after it, when you are aware of its full contents. They consist of four essential components, which in fact correspond to the four major sections of the report.[6] An abstract sets out:
(a) the problem or issue tackled (introduction)
(b) what was done (method)
(c) what was found (results)
(d) the conclusion(s) drawn (conclusion).
The amount said about any of these is strictly limited, because abstracts are usually between 100 and 200 words. There cannot be much more than a single sentence to cover each point. See,

for example, the following, an abstract of a hypothetical experiment introduced earlier (pages 71 to 72), on the borders between social psychology and sociolinguistics.

The study was conducted to see whether Australian speakers tend to make stereotyped judgments on the basis of accent. "Matched guise" versions of a text read in both a Broad and a Cultivated accent were taped and played to forty undergraduates, half of whom were Broad speakers and half Cultivated. All subjects judged the Cultivated accent to be superior on five-point scales of competent/incompetent, intelligent/unintelligent, pleasant/ unpleasant, friendly/unfriendly. The results were the same whether the speakers themselves used Cultivated or Broad accents. It was clear that the Cultivated accent attracts favourable judgments of many kinds, whether the speaker making them normally speaks that way or not. There was no evidence of "accent loyalty".

In this economical statement, all the essential ingredients of the study are reported – the experiment in a nutshell. Yet writing an abstract requires a certain mental adjustment after being involved in writing the report itself. It means distancing yourself from it and trying to see it in terms of its core elements, not its fully developed form. In the abstract the proportions of the report will be changed. The details of the method and the discussion are absent, and the conclusion assumes greater importance beside the other components. The abstract can be reassuring if you were in any doubt as to whether your experiment achieved anything. It will also serve to inform the reader promptly about the contents of your work, just like the other summary devices mentioned in the previous chapter.

. . .

Reports have become the accepted form for presenting the fruits of almost any systematic inquiry. In the offices of government and industry the format varies, and the writers who modify it may or may not know what they are doing. We are all cursed with having to read shapeless "reports" from time to time. But students in science courses have the advantage of a long apprenticeship in using the standard format. They can later adapt it to the demands of the particular task, but without losing touch with the fundamentals, or their reader, in the process.

NOTES

1. "Science only begins when the worker has recorded his results and conclusions in terms intelligible to at least one other person qualified to dispute them." B. M. Couper (1964) cited in H. Dudley, *The Presentation of Original Work in Medicine and Biology* (1977).
2. "Matched guise" involves using the same speaker reading the same piece of text in each of the accents required for the experiment. It demands someone with a talent for imitating other accents.
3. The chemical measured was a constituent of the scale in a boiler.
4. Dudley, pages 13–14.
5. Dudley, page 15.
6. An abstract is sometimes called for in connection with a long essay or a paper in non-science areas. In such cases the work may not be structured according to the standard report format and will not embody the four components. In fact, some sort of summary and synopsis is what is being called for, and these terms are often used interchangeably with abstract, as if they were synonyms.

7

Words and working with them

When people talk of using words, the image often appealed to is that of building. We "construct" statements and "build up" descriptions with words. Words are spoken of as the "foundation stones" or "building blocks" of our communication. The image stops short of saying whether we are building a single structure, or developing whole new streets and suburbs, but it does suggest that writers, like builders, work with prefabricated units to construct something that is greater than the sum of its parts.

The building image, like most analogies, only gets us so far. The prefabricated units of the writer have at least three functions in relation to the whole that are hard to visualize in architectural terms. For one thing, bricks and stones are more-or-less stereotyped components, whereas words are highly differentiated. Words have individual symbolic value, where bricks and stones have it only collectively. A brick or stone is simply itself, while a word signifies something beyond itself.

This capacity of words to refer to aspects of the world around us is their first and most familiar function. Through words (for example *station, trains, crowd, noise*) we can appeal to common experience and communicate the elements of our thinking to others. In technical fields the words on which communication is based are often specialized (for example, *affidavit, disulphides, mitosis, operant conditioning*), and their capacity to symbolize anything to outsiders is very limited. But within the field they are still the signs or symbols on which the exchange of ideas takes place, referring readers to aspects of the discipline and the world. This, then, is the **referential** role of words.

Words, however, have roles other than this, which may be called their **textual** and **interpersonal** roles.[1] The **textual** role is the capacity of words to forge links of meaning with one another in the same text, either within the same sentence or across sentence boundaries.[2] Some kinds of words, for example certain pronouns (*he, she, it, they*), do this regularly; others do so less predictably, depending on the particular piece of writing. The words *building, construct, foundation stones*, etc., in the first paragraph of this chapter, link up as part of a conscious metaphor, just as they would in a text that was really concerned with architecture. But if they were used in phrases that did not consistently exploit the idea of building, as in *image-building, constructing a program,* and *laying the foundation stone*, they would have no textual value for that particular piece.

The **interpersonal** role, meanwhile, is vested in words that make some appeal to the reader. There are words and phrases, for example *clearly, virtually, no doubt, in fact*, that appeal to the reader and are almost entirely interpersonal in their value for the text. They don't interact with the network of referential and textual words around them and could be left out with no loss of meaning. What they do is work on the reader, requesting special attention or endorsement for something. Other interpersonally charged words are less obviously directed at the reader, but they still solicit a particular value judgment along the way. Examples are words such as *careful* and *fussy*. Each invites a judgment (in fact opposite judgments) about the habit of paying attention to detail. The choice of one or the other show how the writer wishes the reader to respond to the information.

A successful piece of writing depends on the interplay of words fulfilling all three of the functions just introduced. This is not as difficult to achieve as it may sound, because many words actually play more than one role. There is both interpersonal and referential value in words like *careful* or *fussy*, and both referential and textual value in words like *one*, as used in the previous sentence. (It refers to a familiar number and also forges a link with the word *three* in the sentence before.) Many textual connections happen spontaneously in writing and do not have to be thought about as you are composing. (To be so concerned with them, then, would probably be inhibiting.) In editing, however, a writer needs to check that there are enough textual connections to make the piece coherent. A check for interpersonal devices should also be made at that later stage.

But let us begin by thinking about the choice of words at the composing stage and those whose role is primarily referential.

REFERENTIAL ROLE OF WORDS

In the act of composing, our search for words is mostly for those that can accurately represent the elements of our message and communicate them reliably to the reader. This generally calls for some thought about the reader's sophistication in the subject and a decision as to how many technical terms we can take for granted.

When writing at the tertiary level, students can assume that the reader is at least as well informed as themselves, and there is no need to shrink from using what is often spoken of, in derogatory terms, as **jargon**. In spite of its negative vibes, jargon is simply the specialized language of a specialized group. It is an economical and imprecise terminology for those in the know. It is viewed unfavourably by those not in the know because they are unable to make anything of it. But within the field it *promotes* communication, as long as it is properly used, and is often taken as a welcome sign of the student's familiarity with theoretical and technical matters. (Cf pages 16 to 18.) There is, however, no point in studding your sentences with technical terms in order to sound impressive. No one will be more aware than the lecturer if you misuse them.

One other point about jargon: because its use is specific to a certain field or discipline, it cannot be transplanted effectively. A student who wants to describe Hamlet's "To be or not to be" problem in terms of "cognitive overload" should think twice before doing so in a literature essay. The point may well fail to communicate, either because the literature lecturer is alienated by the term, or because, like most technical terms, it depends on the company of others from the same field and cannot convey much in isolation. However apt a technical term may seem, outside its home discipline it should be paraphrased in ordinary language.

The use of specialized words, together with the avoidance of colloquial language, makes academic writing rather formal in style. The style is partly a matter of convention, though it is also a by-product of the fundamental seriousness of academic inquiry. Colloquial language would give too casual a tone to a discussion and make the argument seem off-handed and light-weight. To say that Hamlet was considering whether or not to "do himself in" suggests a Monty Python approach that is insensitive to the issues of the play. In other contexts it can be a source of great fun, but it is out of place in literary criticism.

Another problem with colloquialisms is that they are often rather imprecise. In an informal situation the speakers can clarify their meanings, but writing has to communicate without such follow-up, and the choice of words is much more critical. Speakers can and do rely heavily on the thousand most frequently used words in the English vocabulary.[3] Writers, meanwhile, have to draw on the less used resources of standard English in order to express a meaning exactly the first time. These more unusual word choices also tend to set the language of writing apart and make it sound more formal.

The search for specific and exact words is without doubt an important aspect of composing, and it is stressed in almost every handbook on writing and style that you are likely to come across. They urge you to prefer the specific to the general word, or the concrete to the abstract, as a matter of habit. The advice is probably good for those who get into an abstract groove with their word choices (that is, for writers who manifest a tendency towards abstraction and generality!). Such a style loses the reader's attention before long, because there is little to engage with. A *spade* is easier to lay hold of (both physically and mentally) than an *agricultural implement*.

But both kinds of expression are needed in a discussion. The

abstract/general word stands for a much wider category of things, and there are always stages in an argument when you need to look for broader terms of reference. A persistent stream of specifics at the "spade" level (*spade, hoe, rake, trowel, fork, snippers, secateurs* . . .) is as difficult for the reader to absorb as continuous generalities. Unless the miscellaneous specifics are given an explicit cover term, such as *tools*, or *implements*, their collective significance for the discussion is unclear.

General words often play a central part in the development and structure of argument. They connect downwards with the specifics as well as upwards into still higher levels of abstraction. In planning a discussion about the growth of primitive technology, you might well wish to broaden the discussion beyond *tools* and *agricultural implements* to *mechanical aids* generally, and the latter term would give you more room to move in. It enables you to reframe the discussion and makes relevant a wider range of possible topics. (In our example, the term *mechanical aid* would justify our talking about machines as well.)

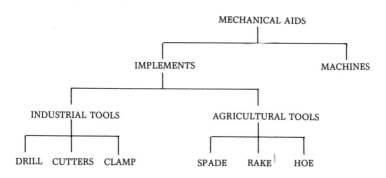

FIGURE 14: A hierarchy of words

In planning a discussion, we need to think in terms of hierarchies of abstraction and to be able to move freely from one level to another. Searching for words at various levels of abstraction is also useful as a way of extending your vocabulary, if that appears to be a problem in any subject.

The degree of abstraction in words is only one of their properties that can be exploited in discussion. Another is their evaluative flavour, which is part of their **connotation**. The connotations of a word are aspects of its meaning that are *implied* in its use (as distinct from the word's core meaning. This is its **denotation**, what it denotes, or refers to). The words *interfere* and *intervene* both refer to the action of involving oneself in the affairs of others (that is, they have a common denotation); yet their connotations are opposite, *intervene* being positively charged and *interfere* negatively. Each puts a particular colouring on the action it is applied to and shows the writer's evaluation of it. It solicits the same evaluation incidentally from the reader, like the words *careful* and *fussy* already mentioned.[4]

The evaluative connotations of words are of considerable importance as you develop an argument or put forth an interpretation of some facts. Just a few are enough to signal your perspective in an otherwise neutral presentation of data. By introducing someone's proposition with the word "claim" or "assert", you imply a real possibility of challenging it and invite the reader to reserve judgment about it, if not to view it sceptically. (Such words are unfortunate if you really mean to endorse the proposition.) But appropriately used they prepare the reader for your counter arguments long before you get to them. By describing a set of predictions in passing as either "optimistic" or "gloomy", you can very simply indicate both your criticism of them and the direction in which you think they err. The connotations of words can provide an interim commentary in a discussion before you communicate the ultimate evaluation or argument.

TEXTUAL ROLE OF WORDS

So far we have been thinking of the choices of words we make in composing a piece of writing and as we try to articulate the argument. The choices made there often contribute to the general cohesiveness of the text, as we have said (see page 87), but this is something to think about at the editing rather than the composing stage. A finished piece of writing must be coherent if it is either to inform or to influence, and this is not simply a matter of having grammatical sentences. Much more, it is providing explicit links between one idea and another, or one point of reference and another, in order to maintain a continuity of meaning throughout the text. It is also an important means of keeping the reader in touch with the ongoing details of your discussion. The reader constantly needs some verbal indication as to what is an extension of what, and how this relates to whatever has gone before.

Textual links are often supplied by the very simple device of **repetition**. Repeating a key word in successive sentences or paragraphs or sections is the most straightforward way to remind your reader of a significant item. This is particularly so in technical or semi-technical writing, where only one word will do. To replace the word *asteroid* with *star* or *heavenly body* would blur the point of reference (they do not mean the same thing for astronomers), so it is simpler and better to repeat *asteroid* itself.

In less technical writing where less hangs on the exactness of the reference, the writer is free to resort to synonyms (that is, words with the same meaning) to keep an idea going. So long as the words have the same denotation and connotation, they will be taken to refer to the same thing. The words *problem* and *difficulty*, used in quick succession, would normally be seen thus, and so remind the reader of a particular focus of attention. They do this in spite of being different words, and have indeed the double advantage of varying the expression while sustaining the reference. The same advantages are to be had by using antonyms (words opposite in meaning), which can also serve as a reminder of a particular point of reference. It seems that we mentally store opposite words together, for example *hot/cold, good/bad, high/low*, and in writing we can rely on the reader to make the connection between a word and its opposite. The word *solution* would certainly be seen to link up (contrastively) with an earlier use of the word *problem*. All such words are chosen first for their referential value, but within a given piece of writing their role is also textual.

Textual spin-off is also to be gained from the relationship

between specific and general words, which we were concerned with on pages 86 to 87. The term *macropod* is the general name for the biological family that kangaroos belong to, and so biologists (and many Australians) would recognize the meaningful link between *kangaroo* and *macropod* if first one and then the other is used in a text. A link would also be seen between either of those and the still broader biological group *marsupials*:

> *"Kangaroo" is the name given to any of the several species of herbivorous mammals of the Australasian region that move by hopping on powerfully developed back legs. In common with other macropods, their forelegs are very short. They are the largest living marsupials in the world . . .*

Because of the interrelationship among the three biological terms, these statements are seen as having a common focus. (Note also the interplay between "the Australasian region" and "the world", marking the writer's supplementary interest in the geographical distributions.) The interplay between general and specific words in those statements contributes to the coherence of the fragmentary text and the continuity of its ideas. As in this small piece, there may be textual value in more than one set of terms in any sequence of sentences, and it all adds to the cohesiveness of the whole.

At the most general end of any scale of English words are the relatively limited number of **all-purpose** words, words such as *activity, aspect, fact, factor, feature, individual, move, procedure, process, sign, thing*, which can be put to use in an enormous range of texts. Like the more abstract words that we were discussing earlier, they allow you to detach yourself one stage further from the specifics, and to broaden the discussion. Unfortunately, they are overused by many writers, and clusters of them are the hallmark of some of the least informative academic and bureaucratic writing. No doubt they are used there to draw a smokescreen over what either cannot or should not be seen for what it is. The following sentence shows how heavy use of such words can obscure a simple idea.

> *There is now official realization of the fact that the individual's predisposition to accept innovation should be a focal aspect of teacher selection procedures . . .*

(In other words: The Department has now caught up with the need to choose teachers who are willing to move with the times!) The extraordinary generality of almost all the words in the "official" version gives them very little power to refer to anything. All-purpose words depend heavily on their more specific neighbours for definition, and they direct our attention on to the accompanying sequences of words (*the fact that* . . . , *an aspect of* . . .), which may or may not supply the needed detail.

When all-purpose words are used in conjunction with more specific vocabulary, they help to make textual links not only within a sentence, but also across sentence boundaries:

Medieval astronomers had no sophisticated telescopes with which to make their observations of the heavens, because glass technology was then still in its infancy. This fact was one of the major obstacles preventing accurate study of planetary movements . . .

The all-purpose word *fact* here stands for a large part of the specific information in the preceding sentence. Through the word *fact* there is a strong textual link between the sentences without any repetition – and it allows the writer to go on with a new idea, that of "obstacles" (perhaps both physical and philosophical), with no sense of discontinuity. In just this way, all-purpose words often serve as junction points in a discussion, enabling writers to move from one preoccupation to another and helping to reorient the reader as they do so.

All-purpose words are just one class of words that can be widely used as substitutes for others more specific. More familiar and much more common are the pronouns (*it, he, she, they*) and their variant forms (*its, his, her, their, him, them*), as well as demonstratives (*this, that, these, those*). (The word *this* alone, without *fact*, could have provided all the necessary connection between the two sentences in the example above.) Words like *another, others, some, one, all, the same*, also replace more specific items and are a neat way of avoiding heavy repetition while making firm textual connections at the same time. All these (!) play a textual role and little else in your writing.

One other group of words that are important textual items are the conjunctives. They are words or phrases that mark the logical connection between complete statements either within a sentence or from one sentence to the next. Some of the commonest are: *and, but, because, if, in fact, however, thus.* The various groups of conjunctives are quite large, and the table below is far from exhaustive. It will nevertheless provide you with some sort of a resource list.

RELATION EXPRESSED	WITHIN SENTENCE	FROM ONE SENTENCE TO THE NEXT
addition	and, and also	also
		in addition
		furthermore
		for instance
	nor	besides
	or, or else	likewise
		in the same way
		similarly
contrast	yet	however
		even so
		nevertheless
	but	instead
		on the contrary
		rather
		by contrast
		otherwise
		on the other hand
		alternatively
		anyhow
		at any rate
		in any case
cause/consequence	because	for this reason
	since	that being so
	for	on account of this
		therefore
	so, so that	as a result
		consequently
		thus
		in that case
		hence

RELATION EXPRESSED	WITHIN SENTENCE	FROM ONE SENTENCE TO THE NEXT
circumstance incl.		
(a) time	(a) when	then
	as	at once
	while	next
		after a while
		meanwhile
		in the meantime
		soon
		now
		at this moment
		hitherto
		up till now
(b) place	(b) where	there
		at that point
		here
		at this point
(c) condition	(c) if	granted
	provided that	that being so
	(al)though	in that case
	even though	under the circumstances
		still
		despite this
		in spite of

TABLE 6: Conjunctives and their roles

As the table shows, there are four kinds of logical relationship that may hold between two successive statements (*addition, contrast, cause/consequence, circumstance*), though each can be further subdivided.[5] At the composing stage you may well be more concerned about the sequencing of statements than with their exact logical relationship with each other. But when reviewing your text at the editing stage, you should check that each conjunctive is appropriate to the content of the statements it connects. If there is a *but* or *however*, do the two statements really contrast with each other? Or is there at least a contrast between the expectations raised by the first statement, and what the second has to say? If *thus* or *therefore* has been used, is the second statement really a consequence of the first? Many writers have a favourite conjunctive and tend to overuse it, perhaps because they think their writing sounds more tightly argued with it. Unfortunately the overuse of any one becomes conspicuous and suspect. As you edit your writing you should check for this and use others from the table of alternatives.

Conjunctives, and all those other words whose role is primarily textual, are among the least noticeable in a piece of writing, yet they contribute much to the readability and communicative efficiency of your text. The following fragment from *The New English Bible* shows skilful use of both a pronoun and a conjunctive:

> The kingdom of Heaven is like mustard-seed, which a man took and sowed in his field. As a seed, mustard is smaller than any other; but when it has grown it is bigger than any garden-plant; it becomes a tree, big enough for the birds to come and roost among its branches . . .

In this the pronoun *it* serves as a focus for a set of statements, drawing them together and linking them with the earlier reference to *mustard*. The conjunctive *but* prepares for the (relative) unexpectedness of what follows and marks the balance of statement and counter-statement. As in any longer piece of text, it also marks the boundary between statements supporting one point and those that support another. A careful writer will thus advise the reader of any coming shift in the discussion.

INTERPERSONAL ROLE OF WORDS

In the preceding pages we have already noted from time to time how words can indirectly aid the reader in responding to a piece of writing. But writers may also appeal directly to the reader through a number of devices that we may call **interpersonal**. These devices are not part of the referential content of the text, and if you left them out it would still communicate the same essential ideas. But they are quite important in influencing your reader's response to particular points and in disposing him or her to share your views as far as possible.

One simple way of appealing to readers is to confront them

with questions, commands or exclamations, which, as in normal conversation, solicit some kind of reply. The exchanges of normal conversation are also suggested by the use of *I* or *we* and addressing the reader directly as *you*. In informal writing, for example personal letters, these things are very common, and it is often tempting to use them in academic writing. But some departments come down heavily on the use of *I*, probably because it is felt to be a symptom of subjective thinking when students should be working with objective evidence. To downplay any personal involvement, the *I* has traditionally been excluded in reports of scientific experiments. Students are obliged to say:

50 g of potassium bromide was placed in a flask and heated . . .
rather than
I put 50 g of potassium bromide in a flask and heated it . . .
(You might like to consider whether the latter wording could possibly misrepresent what was done or mislead anyone who wanted to repeat the experiment.) In fact it seems that professional scientists are beginning to accept more personally worded accounts of research,[6] and some scientific journals (notably biological journals published in the U.S.A.) now actually encourage their contributors to write in a more direct, personal fashion. But the use of *I* is still frowned on in many departments, and perhaps it is best to play safe and avoid it.

There are in any case plenty of other interpersonal devices that are perfectly acceptable in more formal writing. One such involves converting what would have been the verb in a more personal form of expression: *I was surprised/amazed/disappointed at the findings of . . .* into an adjective, thus: *the surprising/ amazing/disappointing findings of . . . .* The revised wording would of course require some adjustments to the grammar of the sentence, but it would still communicate the character of your feeling without making it overtly personal. Comparable adverbs (*surprisingly/disappointingly*) can also be used to express and evoke a personal response, and are fully accepted in traditional scientific writing,[7] as in *The results were surprisingly high.* These interpersonal words are not essential to a plain description of your material, but they help to keep readers in touch with your perspective on it and indicate points at which you would hope for some intellectual response from them, preferably endorsing your point of view! The words' role is evaluative, like some of those we discussed earlier (page 88), which combine evaluation with their referential function.

Other kinds of interpersonal words are those that can be dropped into a discussion to express your confidence or reservations and doubts about something. With them you would hope to arouse the same attitude in your reader, and you can but try. Your confidence can be communicated by any of the numerous *emphatic* and *absolute* words, such as *clearly, certainly, undoubtedly, always*, or words that both isolate and give special stress to something, such as *central, crucial, fundamental, major, principal*. Your reservations can be communicated through "hedge" words of varying degrees, ranging from *possibly, perhaps, apparently*, to *usually, probably, generally*. Downright scepticism comes across with *allegedly* or *supposedly*. All these attitudes can be expressed at greater length through equivalent phrases:

possibly   it is possible that
generally   as a general rule

Some writers make extensive use of these devices in order to underline a point of view, or else to cover themselves against sounding over-assertive or being caught out on their facts. But, like any stylistic device, it soon becomes conspicuous and loses its strategic value. Moderate and varied use is the best advice, and also to express attitudes from time to time through the connotations of words whose first role is referential. Instead of using *supposedly*, you could, for instance, make use of the word *claim*, discussed earlier (page 88). Thus the sentence:

Violence seen on TV is supposedly a stimulus to violent behaviour . . .

could be rewritten as:

Some researchers have claimed that violence seen on TV is a stimulus to violent behaviour . . .

Like the emphatic and absolute words of the last paragraph, *negatives* can serve to convey a confident point of view, as in:

There is no empirical support for the theory

or

None of the answers is satisfactory.

Curiously, negative elements can also be employed as a means of softening an assertion or uncomfortable fact. So the writer who says:

The Chamber of Commerce was not ready to discuss the effects of pollution on the river . . .

puts it more tactfully than the one who says:

The Chamber of Commerce refused to discuss the effects of pollution on the river . . .

Negative prefixes, for example *dis-, in-/im-, non-, un-,* attached to a word can also seem to soften the thrust of a comment and make it more acceptable than a simple synonym. See, for example, *disrespectful* v. *rude,* or *improbable* v. *crazy.* But, once again, the technique offers diminishing returns, and its overuse within a sentence can generate total confusion. What, for example, does the following mean?

The authors are not disinclined to admit the improbability of the eventual non-participation of anti-bodies in the reaction.

The reader can only assume that whatever it says doesn't matter, and read on!

Finally, there is interpersonal value in words that guide the reader as to the overall structure of your text. It is helpful to mark the individual points or units of your discussion in some way, either by formal enumeration, that is, *first(ly), second(ly), third(ly),* or a more informal system, using such words and phrases as *first of all, then, next, a further issue, finally.* The formal system has the virtue and vice of a catalogue. It imposes a clear order but no rationale on the items it presents, and it leaves with the reader the obligation to find some meaningful interrelationship among them. This, of course, is really the writer's obligation and should be thought about in the light of some of the suggestions in chapter 3. The other problem with formal enumeration is that it is open-ended, as congregations listening to the traditional long-winded preacher well know.

With the informal system the writer makes less of the overall inventory of points, and more of the transitions between them. This is usually enough, as long as there is a clear underlying rationale in the choice of individual points and in their sequence. The reader simply needs a signal to know when you are moving from point to point, so as to recognize the structure of your argument or discussion. Such signals are particularly important at the beginning of a paragraph, where readers are predisposed to receive a change or new development of the topic. The reader will be grateful for confirmation of this, either through such words as *next, also, in addition,* or through some other transitional comment, perhaps indicating whether the discussion is about to become broader or more specific. An example of the former would be:

> *The hygiene problem outlined in the previous paragraph is just one of a number of medical and social issues raised by . . .*

and of the latter:

> *Many of the prophecies of Nostradamus seem to have come true in the twentieth century. For example . . .*

The writer can often take advantage of the interplay between general and specific words (or the other way round) in transitional comments. They help to articulate the structure of the discussion, as we have already seen, and incidentally help to keep the reader in touch with it. Anything you can do to reassure your reader that you are in command of the discussion is worth doing.

Choosing words is thus more than a matter of finding the ones to express your ideas. Well-chosen words interact with one another to make your text cohesive, to mark the individual components and structure of your discussion, and to keep your reader in close touch with it at every stage. For all these things we have the rich resources of English to draw upon.

NOTES

1. The terms are those of M. A. K. Halliday. See, for instance, *Explorations in the Functions of Language* (Edward Arnold, London, 1973), ch. 2.
2. The words within a sentence are, of course, also interrelated by the grammar, but that is not our concern in this chapter.
3. See, for example, *A Study of the Oral Vocabulary of Adults,* by F. Schonell, I. Meddleton and B. Shaw (Univ. of Queensland Press, 1956), p. 63.
4. Evaluative words make demands of the reader, just as value words (in the question) make demands of the writer. Cf pp. 18 to 19.

5. See *Cohesion in English*, by M. A. K. Halliday and R. Hasan (Longman, London, 1976).
6. "Judicious" use of personal pronouns was a feature of the texts most highly rated in a study reported in *Good Style for Scientific and Engineering Writing* by J. Kirkman (Pitman, London, 1980).
7. See *Scientific Text*, by Peter Roe, in *Discourse Analysis Monographs* no. 4 (Birmingham University, 1977), p. 33.

8

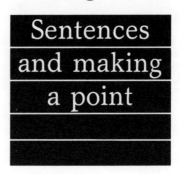

Sentences and making a point

Though we use them all the time, sentences are far from easy to define. Linguists themselves have trouble finding a definition that will cover the immense variety of sentences used in speech and writing. Even if we confine our discussion to written sentences, there is plenty of variety and no single typical form. Many people would fall back on the idea that a sentence is the sequence of words between one full stop and the next. But this is small help when you want to produce reliable sentences in your writing.

Broadly speaking, what any sentence does is to make a point or a statement. In writing, that point or statement has to be communicated fully and explicitly if it is to inform or influence the reader; and this means that sentences need to be constructed with a good deal of care. Both the length and internal structure of sentences can be adapted, within certain limits, to serve the point you wish to put across. So the form of individual sentences will be the concern of the first part of this chapter. It will involve a little grammar, but no more than is needed to identify the different kinds of sentences you would want to have at your fingertips.

Beyond the question of what goes into individual sentences is the problem of managing them collectively – making sure that a well-expressed point doesn't get lost among the sentences surrounding it. This means controlling the information focus in successive sentences, an issue that will take up the latter part of the chapter. It will lead us finally to the issue of paragraphing.

Few writers are able to think at the same time about the contents of individual sentences and how they work collectively. Again, you might tackle these two things at different stages: the matter of individual sentences as you compose, and the information focus as you edit. Some thought about both will contribute to the effectiveness of your ultimate discussion.

INDIVIDUAL SENTENCES: their form and structure

Probably the most obvious thing about the construction of sentences is their length. We are all very conscious of the long sentence that keeps adding in extra details to colour and flavour a point, but in doing so keeps adding to its sheer bulk, too, so that it becomes difficult to swallow and is bound to be a strain on the reader's mental digestion! Like antacid tablets, the short sentence gives welcome relief. Brief is beautiful, at least now and then.

Longer sentences are generally more difficult to construct, and for this reason students may be encouraged to keep the length of their sentences down. Some books suggest that twenty-five words is beginning to be a lot and that you should aim for fewer than that. But this is only a rough guide; longer sentences can be perfectly readable if well constructed, and shorter ones can be difficult because of their own internal problems. Matters of vocabulary and internal structure interact with length to produce more (or less) readable sentences.

The following sentence consists of less than twenty-five words:

This feline celebrity, by an act of rodent elimination, has contributed to the security of the edible assets of the property constructed by Jack.

But it communicates rather poorly because of the heavy vocabulary loosely strung together in phrases. Yet the old nursery rhyme that it translates is not comfortable reading either:

This is the cat that killed the rat that ate the malt that lay in the house that Jack built.

The vocabulary here is simple enough, but the structure is unbalanced. The string of *that* statements distract attention from the sentence's main focus: the cat. Neither sentence communicates very well, though neither exceeds twenty-five words. The problem is that each embodies too many ill-assorted facts, and this is really what makes a sentence seem badly managed or too long.

Ideally, your sentences don't draw attention to themselves as being either long or short. They are just a suitable size and shape for the information that has to be communicated. If you seem to have trouble with longer sentences, you should aim to reduce the number of *ideas* you try to get into each one, not just cut down on the number of words. Sentences can and should vary in length depending on how much they have to convey.

Shorter or longer sentences will result from the way you package your ideas for delivery to the reader. The packaging should reflect the structure of your ideas, so that the ones that you feel belong together are in the same sentence and independent ones are set apart across a sentence boundary. In a short sentence you effectively isolate an idea from others:

(a) *The book's contents are innovative. They are also attractively presented, with plenty of visual aids.*

But in

(b) *The book's contents are innovative and are presented attractively, with plenty of visual aids . . .*

the two ideas are joined up into a longer sentence and make a more integrated comment on the book. The disappearance of the word *they* is a grammatical sign of this integration. In (a), meanwhile, the two points are made independently. Each is given individual attention, although the first seems to give way entirely to the second across the sentence boundary, and the ongoing focus of attention is the book's presentation, not its contents. A short sentence may thus be used to "get something out of the way".

Length isn't the only thing that will vary in the sentences you use to put your ideas on paper. Sentences may be constructed in three ways, often called **simple**, **compound** or **complex**.

A combination of the last two, **compound/complex**, makes a fourth.[1] We have already been looking at examples of the simple and compound types in the preceding paragraph, where both sentences in (a) were straightforward examples of the simple sentence, and (b) was a compound sentence.

The simple sentence consists of just two parts, called the **subject** (what or who the statement is about), and **predicate** (what is actually said about it/him/her/them.) The **subject and predicate unit** is the core of any statement, and the structure of any sentence can be analysed in terms of

(a) the number of S(-ubject) + P(-redicate) units.
and
(b) the interrelationship between these units.

A simple sentence consists of one S + P unit, while the compound one has two (or more), usually linked by *and, yet, but, so, for, or,* or *nor.*

In a compound sentence the two (or more), S + P units become equal links in a continuous chain. They are normally independent observations, each of which could stand alone in a simple sentence. The compound sentence joins them up as if each was as important as the other. This is where the difference between compound and complex sentences lies, for **complex** sentences link two or more S + P units in an unequal relationship. It is a hierarchy with at least two levels, depending on the number and nature of the units. One unit is elevated to the status of chief point, and the other(s) made subordinate or dependent. For instance:

(a) *The book will communicate well **because it is attractively presented.***

(b) *This book, **which is attractively presented**, will communicate well.*

(c) *A book communicates well **when it is attractively presented.***

(d) *The book shows **how presentation enhances communication.***

(e) *A book **that is attractively presented** will communicate well.*

The words in bold type in each sentence form a subordinate

point, one that is presented as the condition or circumstance under which the chief statement (not in bold type) holds good. The examples use only a handful of the various connective words (*because, which, when, how, that*) that couple together the units of a complex sentence. Some others are listed in the table on pages 92 to 93, but there are many more.

Each of the three major sentence types has its particular communicative role in writing. The simple sentence, as already seen, helps to isolate one point amid longer sentences. The compound sentence allows you to prepackage two or more similar points with a minimum of fuss, and delivers their respective messages efficiently. Yet a long run of compound sentences may turn the reader off, since they deliver information in a relatively unstructured and seemingly assertive way. Each unit of the sentence is of equal importance and makes equal claim on the reader's attention.

Complex sentences, meanwhile, will structure your points into a hierarchy because they automatically set up a chief point and make the rest dependent on it. The relationship between the chief point and the rest can be of several kinds. It may express the condition or circumstances under which the chief statement holds, as in (c), or an underlying cause or reason, as in (a); it may add descriptive details as in (b), or definitive detail to either subject or object, as in (e) and (d). One way or another, they underpin the chief statement and deepen the discussion. Their more varied structures bring elegance to a writer's style.

But with too many types of subordination in a single sentence you may find yourself with a boa-constrictor that threatens to strangle the message. Even professional writers sometimes struggle to manage their complex sentences, like the judge who wrote:

> *Every avenue **that has been followed in seeking to identify intervention by W. in the protection or assistance of H.** has ended, **in so far as a path to W. is concerned**, not merely inconclusively, but specifically in his favour.*

This is hardly a comfortable sentence to read, with its two subordinate statements (in bold type) interrupting the flow of the main statement. A complex sentence is certainly easier on the reader when the chief statement in it is left intact. The subordinate statements are better placed either before or after the chief statement, and after is best if there are two or three of them. Yet some kinds of subordinate statement occur more often than others in the before position, in particular those dealing with conditions (usually introduced by *if, unless, although,* etc.) or with time (introduced by *when, as, while,* etc.). Such statements usually provide an important context for the reading of the chief statement, and in the before position they become the "topic unit" in the ongoing discussion. (Cf page 107.)

MANAGING THE FOCUS

In a single sentence it is easy enough to get the emphasis where you want it. But in sequences of sentences there are many points clamouring for attention and the writer must introduce them strategically to control their demands, ensure an even flow of information, and maintain the continuity of ideas. Too many new ideas at once make for difficult reading and possibly incoherence.

Any normal sentence in a continuous text contains a blend of older and newer information. It will focus on something that is the same as or clearly related to a topic already raised; and it will make some fresh comment about it. In those terms the information structure of a sentence may sound rather like its grammatical structure, as we described it earlier under the labels subject and predicate (page 103). Yet the **topic** of a sentence, as we shall now call it, does not always correspond to its grammatical subject, nor the **comment** to its predicate. They do happen to coincide in:

Subject	**Predicate**
The book's contents	*are innovative.*
(topic)	(comment)

Things are different if the sentence is slightly modified:

In comparison with others, the book's contents are innovative.
Here the topic is the whole of the first phrase ("in comparison with others") and all the rest becomes the comment. Thus the terms **topic** and **comment** for our present purposes refer to

relative positions in the sentence: the advanced position, and the remainder. These two positions are crucial for the management of information in continuous writing. What comes in the advanced position (unless it is an interpersonal element – see pages 94 to 98) is received as the matter currently under discussion, and what follows as information about it. We will be calling the material in the topic the **topic unit**, and that in the comment the **comment unit**.

Most of the time the topic unit is something that has already been introduced. In the topic position it becomes activated as the current focus of attention. Attention may well become diffused as any discussion develops, and the topic position can and should be used to keep the reader on the track. The wording of the topic unit is therefore quite important. You can reactivate a familiar unit in its original terms, or paraphrase it (*this book/this publication*) to maintain the focus while varying the expression. You can also use the topic position to redescribe something mentioned earlier (*this account of x*), in order to adjust the reader's perspective on something for future discussion. Whatever its verbal form, the topic position confirms that it is the ongoing focus of interest.

Because the topic position is so important, writers need to be able to manoeuvre things into it, and there are a number of ways of doing this. It can be done with a *topicalizing phrase*, as in our modified sentence above. There are numerous carrier phrases for you to adapt to the topical needs of the moment, for example:

From the practical point of view, the service cannot . . .
　　　　theoretical
　　　　historical
or
　In a similar study, Brown found that . . .
　　　smaller
　　　later
Standard topicalizing phrases can become tiresome, however, and are sometimes used unnecessarily, as in:
　As to the question of finance, it will be generated by public appeal.
Assuming that the matter of finance is already under discus-

sion, this could be better and more simply expressed as:

The finance will be generated by public appeal.

The word *finance* is the topic anyway, so it needs no topicalizing.

There are, of course, other alternatives to the topicalizing phrase. A whole subordinate statement can be added to topicalize the necessary point. Instead of saying:

In comparison with others, the book's contents are innovative

we could topicalize the matter of comparisons thus:

When you compare it with others, the book's contents are innovative.

This incidentally turns that sentence from a simple to a complex one. It helps to vary the sentence grammar, as well as avoiding the standard phrase.

Switching from active to passive (or vice versa) is another way of manoeuvring something into topic position. The terms *active* and *passive* refer to two different forms of a verb, a difference that may be illustrated by the following pairs of sentences:

He wrote the book in a hurry. (active)

The book was written in a hurry. (passive)

The prime minister welcomed the news. (active)

The news was welcomed by the prime minister. (passive)

The statements with the active verb have subjects who (that) perform an action or actively register a perception, whereas those with passive verbs have subjects that are the products or passive objects of the activity of the verb. The use of passive constructions is often criticized as contributing to dull and unnecessarily complicated writing, and the criticism is probably just when a writer offers no relief from passive constructions. The active is more direct, other things being equal, and may be easier for the reader to process.[2]

But, as already indicated, the passive can help to move items in and out of topic position. Both sentences in the pairs above express the same point while they topicalize different items. The writer's choice between them would depend on what needed to be activated for discussion. If, taking the second pair, the P.M.'s response was the focus of interest, the active statement would topicalize this for ongoing discussion:

*(The defence forces today announced their decision to amalga-
mate.) The P.M. welcomed the news. He called a press confer-
ence to discuss security issues . . .*

The passive version of the same statement would topicalize an
ongoing interest in the character of the news itself:

*(The defence forces today announced their decision to amalga-
mate.) The news was welcomed by the P.M. Its value for national
security was favourably commented on in the press . . .*

The topicalizing you can achieve with the passive verb is well
integrated with the sentence itself, effective and relatively
unobtrusive.

An occasional use of the passive verb as a means of topicalizing will hardly attract attention, because passive verbs are so
widely used in academic writing for other reasons. They are
the conventional means of avoiding personal reference and give
an objective veneer to a dubiously objective point, as when a
writer uses: *It was felt that* . . . rather than *I think* . . . , or *It
was discovered* . . . rather than *We found* . . . . But the habit
seems to carry over even into references to a third party, and
many report writers, as they review the earlier literature, are
inclined to say:

It was found (Brown, 1977) that children exposed to . . .

not

Brown (1977) found that children exposed to . . .

The *it* has no topical value in the first of these, and the direct
and concise wording of the second seems preferable.

The passive wording of statements is a normal feature of
scientific writing, and several reasons probably combine to
institutionalize it there.[3] One is the desire to maintain objec-
tivity and avoid imputing causes where they would be a matter
of speculation. Another is the desire to play down personal
involvement in experimental routines, since the involvement
is irrelevant to the procedures being carried out. The same
procedures carried out by anyone in the class would, or should,
produce the same results. In fact it is the procedures and
processes themselves that are the focus of attention, and the
passive verbs with their impersonal subjects help to highlight
and topicalize them. This probably explains why, according to

one study,[4] more passive constructions occurred in a sampling of chemistry texts than in an equivalent number of physics and biology texts.

TOPICAL PROGRESSION

So far we have talked as if maintaining a particular focus is the most important aspect of managing sequences of sentences. At times it certainly is, as when you want to introduce a set of comments relating to a single matter:

> *This book is a remarkable contribution to Australian social history. It presents within its pages people from many walks of life and three generations. It is constructed so as to illuminate a significant number of Australian institutions . . .*

In diagram form,[5] the information in these sentences is presented thus:

SENTENCE 1.   Topic unit 1 – Comment unit 1
SENTENCE 2.   T.u.1 – C.u.2
SENTENCE 3.   T.u.1 – C.u.3

FIGURE 15: *Topical progression pattern 1*

The subject of the first sentence (*the book*) stays (as *it*) in the topic position of the sentences that follow, keeping the spotlight on it.

But unless we change the focus from time to time, our discussion will go nowhere. What we often do is to bring into topic position something from the preceding comment, moving the discussion along in a progression that, when diagrammed, looks like the steps of a staircase:

SENTENCE 1.   Topic unit 1 – Comment unit 1
SENTENCE 2.   T.u.2 – C.u.2
SENTENCE 3.   T.u.3 – C.u.3

FIGURE 16: *Topical progression pattern 2*

This is the topical progression in:

> *The book is set in a small Australian country town. The place has a Victorian character, but it might be any within 150 kilometres of an eastern capital city. Regular contact with the city is part of the lifestyle of most of the population . . .*

The focus here passes smoothly from one thing to another, from "the book" to "the place" to its urban contacts, the second and third topic units activating elements from the preceding comments. In each case the topic units selects from it, and/or redescribes it, thus providing verbal variety as well as introducing other perspectives (narrower, wider, or just different) on the matter under discussion. Both the redescription and the movement of the topical focus help the discussion along.

From time to time a single comment will supply more than one item for development (comment unit a, b, . . . etc.), in a progression that is known as the "split comment". Diagrammed, the pattern looks like this:

SENTENCE 1. Topic unit 1 − Comment unit 1(a) and 1(b)
SENTENCE 2. T.u.2 − C.u.2
SENTENCE 3. T.u.3 − C.u.3

FIGURE 17: Topical progression pattern 3

This pattern is the one underlying:

> *The book's account of an Australian country town is both true-to-life and artistically constructed. A set of interviews provided the author with material for each chapter, interviews with both older and younger residents. But artful rearrangement of this material disguises the means by which it was collected . . .*

The main topical progression in these sentences is from the split comment of the first sentence to the topics of the second and third sentences. But we might also note the interplay between the comment of the second sentence and the topic of the third (in the word *material*). Both topic and comment tend to become more elaborate in academic writing, and as they do there may be more than one topical connection in a sequence of sentences. Supplementary links of this kind help to bind the discussion together more tightly.

Sometimes the topical progression is set up through several components of a whole (for example, *head, eyes, nose, chin*, in a portrait) or related aspects of a broader and more generalized topic unit. The concept that integrates these components or aspects may itself remain implicit, as in the following:

*In the past, the townspeople drew on the surrounding country-
side for their livelihoods. The population nowadays is mostly
employed in decentralized industries, or else makes a living on
the highway by transport-driving. The future township will show
few traces of its rural connections . . .*

The underlying pattern of progression is:

SENTENCE 1. Topic unit 1(i) – Comment unit 1
SENTENCE 2.   T.u.1(ii) – C.u.2
SENTENCE 3.   T.u.1(iii) – C.u.3

FIGURE 18: Topical progression pattern 4

In the illustrative sentences above, the individual topic units
connect with one another through a generalized notion of time.
The association of past with present and future on a broad time-
scale is familiar enough to support the topical progression and
ensure that each sentence is seen as relevant to the others. Such
generalized notions can be vested in common experience, as
here, or in more specialized knowledge that the writer can
assume the reader shares.

The patterns of topical progression are not likely to be upper-
most in your mind as you compose your discussion, but it is
worth checking for them as you review and edit your work,
particularly when there seems to be a "sticky patch" in which
the argument gets bogged down.

Sticky patches quite often result from problems in the use
of the topic and comment, either within a sentence or in the
ongoing sequence of sentences. Sometimes the first draft
sentence is one in which the topic annexes material that should
be left for the comment. The following rather top-heavy
sentence shows this problem:

*The author's masterly account of an Australian country town in
transition impresses the reader.*

The sentence puts all its goods in front, and tails off weakly,
leaving the writer nothing to go on with. The cure is to reduce
the topic unit thus:

*The author gives a masterly account of an Australian country
town in transition.*

This revised version of the sentence is better balanced, and provides a lead in the comment for future development.

A sticky patch may, on the other hand, be caused by too great a leap in the topical progression. If a vital step is left out it makes the discussion elliptical and harder to follow. It may also seem illogical, even though there is reasonable logic underlying it. The cure, again, is to check the topical progressions within the "patch" to see that all the connections are explicit. The missing link could be supplied by any of the following:

(a) redistribution of the material in the topic and comment;
(b) redescription of the ongoing topic unit; or
(c) an additional sentence.

Alternatively, it may be time for a new paragraph . . .

FROM SENTENCES TO PARAGRAPHS

Looking into your topical progressions has one further benefit. It helps to answer the sometimes vexed question as to where paragraphs should begin and end.

Paragraphs are elusive things to define, and this naturally makes them difficult units to identify. Traditionally they are said to be "a unit of thought", although this definition might seem to apply equally to the contents of one sentence, or a whole set of them. (How big is "a thought"?) It varies, of course, but paragraphs normally consist of more than one sentence, because they embody not just the statement of the thought, but some sort of exploration of it. (Our daily newspapers are an exception to this, but their one-sentence paragraphs are at least partly a response to the narrow columns of print.) On a full-width page the typical paragraph consists of several sentences that sustain and explore a particular thought. They form a group by virtue of their common focus of interest.

When groups of sentences concentrate on describing a single entity (for example a publication or a theory) you would probably expect them to show a topical progression like patterns 1 or 4 above. You might then expect to find whole paragraphs consisting of just those patterns. In fact this is not so common. Even the dominant topic unit is commonly introduced as the comment of the first sentence (as in the example below), and so pattern 2 (or 3) would also be involved. Most paragraphs consist of more than one of the patterns shown above. So the patterns themselves do not define paragraphs for us. Rather, we must investigate how the patterns interlock in a set of sentences, and where there are breaks in the chain. The right paragraphing for the following sentences can be decided in just this way. (The topics are in bold type.)

Section 90 of the Australian Constitution prevents the states from charging excise. It is both a peculiarity of our Constitution, and something of a mystery. No other major federation bans its states from taxing goods. In the U.S. each of the states has its own retail sales tax. The same goes for India, Canada and so on. No one seems to know why the ban on state excise was inserted in the Constitution. Perhaps, it has been argued, it was to reinforce the federal government's customs powers. The recent High Court decision reaffirms what economists call the vertical fiscal imbalance in this country: most of the money spent by state and federal governments is raised by the federal government alone.

The topical progressions involved here are of all four kinds, but tracing them shows that the first seven sentences belong together, and the eighth is the start of the new paragraph.

SENTENCE 1. T.u.1 – C.u.1
SENTENCE 2. T.u.2 – C.u.2(a) and 2(b)(i)
SENTENCE 3. T.u.3 – C.u.3
SENTENCE 4. T.u.3 – C.u.4
SENTENCE 5. T.u.4 – C.u.5
SENTENCE 6. T.u.5(ii) – C.u.6
SENTENCE 7. T.u.5(iii) – C.u.7
SENTENCE 8. T.u.1 – C.u.1 . . .

FIGURE 19: A combination of topical progressions

The first seven sentences are all concerned with the general practice of "preventing states from charging excise". They inquire how widespread it is and why it should exist in Australia. The eighth sentence marks a new point of departure. It introduces a related subject, but its topic has no particular connection with the previous topical progressions. The discontinuity is where the new paragraph should begin.

The paragraph (sentences 1 to 7) that we have just identified makes good use of its first sentence to announce its focus of interest. This is especially important in academic writing because it can range so widely, and readers need to know with the start of each paragraph what is currently under the spotlight. The sentence that does this has traditionally been called the "topic sentence", an expression that is awkward for us, since we have been applying the word *topic* to a position in individual sentences, not what a whole paragraph is about. To avoid confusion, let us rename the "topic sentence" the **index sentence**, though its role is exactly the same: to indicate to the reader what the paragraph is "on about". As in our paragraph (sentences 1 to 7), the topical progression often leads off from the comment of the index sentence rather than its topic. But as long as the lead is provided in either position of the index sentence, it will serve the reader well. Every paragraph should have one.

We have spent some time discussing sentences as individuals and as members of groups. As individuals they are very malleable, but any change you make to a sentence can affect its relations with its neighbours. Whenever you modify a sentence you will need to check that it still works in the continuous flow of sentences and that the necessary topical progressions are there. By keeping such things in mind, you can ensure that your writing is both flexible and effective in making its point.

NOTES

1. *Compound/complex* sentences involve at least two statements coordinated by *and, but, or,* etc., as well as at least one subordinate statement. See further pp. 103 and 105.
2. On the processing of passives, see "Some psychological studies of grammar", an article by G. A. Miller in *American Psychologist*, 17 (1962), pp. 748–62.
3. G. W. Turner, "On the passive construction in English scientific writing", *Australian Universities Modern Languages Association Journal*, 17 (1962), pp. 181–197.
4. R. Huddleston, R. Hudson, E. Winter and A. Henrici, *Sentence and Clause in Scientific English* (Communication Research Centre, University College London, 1968), p. 653.

5. My debt to George Dillon, *Constructing Texts* (Indiana University Press, 1981), pp. 106-9, and Frantisek Danes, *Functional Sentence Perspective* (Mouton, The Hague, 1974), pp. 118-120, is evident in the diagrams used here.

9

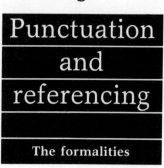

Punctuation and referencing

The formalities

The dots and spots of punctuation are often thought of as places where you "take a breath". In speaking or reading aloud, there are always pauses between groups of words, and they serve the double purpose of giving *you* time to recharge your lungs, and your listener time to digest the words you have just communicated. In silent reading the breath supply doesn't matter, but the reader can still only take in a group of words at a time and needs regular mental breaks. No one can process words continuously.

Our punctuation serves to mark the breaks between sentences as well as between units within individual sentences. (There is also punctuation for individual words, and this, too, will be covered in the notes below.) The major breaks between sentences are of course made by full stops, question marks and exclamation marks, while lesser breaks within the sentence are made by such marks as commas, colons and semicolons. The various marks often indicate something about the status of the preceding string of words or the relationship between those before and after, as we shall see. There are nevertheless only a few hard and fast rules about punctuation these days, and writers have a good deal of freedom and usually some options to exercise. The most general rule to bear in mind is that you punctuate to clarify the meaning of your words for the reader.

Some punctuation marks help you to make distinctions that cannot be made at all in spoken language. The apostrophe does this in *the programme's quality* v. *the programmes' quality*. Other punctuation marks help to sort out relationships among written words that would be clear enough if they were spoken. The intonation patterns of speech serve, among other things, to group words into relevant subsets, but this has to be achieved by other means in writing. Without punctuation, the even spaces between each written word invite the eye to wander continuously on to the next and can promote misreading. It can happen even in a short sentence:

Had they gone on the track would have led them over a cliff.

Λ comma is badly needed after the word "on" to show what goes with what and to ensure correct reading first time. The longer the sentence, the more likely it is that some internal punctuation will be needed to clarify the meaning.

Because punctuation interacts with the meaning of sentences and words it can hardly be regarded as a ⁻ᵤrely "cosmetic" aspect of writing. It makes for good relations with readers by indicating where they can take their mental breaks, and preventing misreadings, which waste their time. Occasionally a writer overpunctuates, but much more often the problem is one of underpunctuation, and it is one of the several things to check as you edit your work. It is best done two or three days after the first full draft, when you can no longer "hear" the sentences you composed and take them for granted. Then you will be able to read them more critically, as if they were someone else's. Only then will you pick up the occasions when one string of words runs out of control into the next.

Both word and sentence punctuation marks are elements of correct referencing, and so our chapter concludes with some notes on that also.

WORD PUNCTUATION

1. APOSTROPHE

(a) To precede the possessive *s* ending in phrases that mark possession (for example *the man's clothes*) or some inalienable relationship (for example *the man's departure*). When the possessing word already ends in a plural *s*, the apostrophe alone is added, as in *the programmes' quality*. When the possessing word is singular but ends in *s*, it is now usual to add both apostrophe and possessive *s*, for example, *David Jones's windows*. Some writers, however, maintain the custom of using the apostrophe alone after a final *s* if the word is a classical, literary or biblical name, for example *Achilles' heel, Jesus' teachings*.

Note: An apostrophe is **not** used in the possessive *its*, because *it's* is the contracted form of *it is*. (See (b)). It may help to remember that possessive *its* is exactly like *hers, ours, yours, theirs*, none of which has an apostrophe.

(b) To mark the omission of one or more letters from a word, as in *don't, isn't, it's, wouldn't*. Contracted forms like these, however, are considered by some to be too informal for academic writing.

2. HYPHEN

(a) To link the two parts of a compound when it is in danger of being misconstrued. For example, *bacteria carrying dust particles* needs a hyphen between the first two words to convey the meaning intended. The use of hyphens in established compounds is far from standardized: British and American practice has diverged (see Ernest Gowers' edition of Fowler's *Modern English Usage* (Oxford University Press, 1965)), and dictionaries differ. This frees writers from any conventional obligations with hyphens but leaves with them the responsibility of deciding when they are necessary to clarify meaning, as in the example above.

(b) To link the two parts of a word that has to be divided because of lack of space at the end of a line. The division should be made at a syllable break, for example *acknowledg - ment*, not *acknowle - dgment, nor acknowledgme - nt*. It is preferable to have a consonant as the first letter after the hyphen, as in *combina - tion*, except where this would mean interfering with the root of the word, as it would in *drawing* (*dra - wing* would be an unfortunate way to divide such a word).

118

3. INVERTED COMMAS (SEE ALSO QUOTATION MARKS, PAGE 122)

(a) To set apart foreign words or phrases, for example "carabinieri", "coup de grâce".

(b) To set apart words under discussion, as in: *the term "justice" is rarely neutral* . . . Many writers now use underlining, instead of inverted commas, to set words apart.

Note: When discussing a literary work, the title should be set apart from the ordinary run of words. By convention, the titles of individual poems or essays are set in inverted commas, while the title of a collection or a whole work is underlined. For example, "Ode to a Grecian Urn", and Songs of Innocence and Experience or Paradise Lost.

4. STOPS

To show that a word has been abbreviated, for example *cont., ref., vol., Fri., N.S.W., J. R. Lyons.* There is, however, an increasing tendency to omit the stops in the abbreviations of well-known organizations such as *NATO, ILO, NRMA, ACTU.* Stops are not used in the short forms of commonly used terms of quantity (for example *99c*), for ordinals (*2nd*), for compass points (*NNE*), or for SI units (*kg, ha, mm, °C*).

5. OBLIQUE (OR SLASH) MARK

To indicate optional readings at a particular point, for example *he/she.*

Sentence Punctuation

A. Major breaks – between one sentence and the next

1. FULL STOP

To mark the end of a sentence, for example:

The king is dead.

or

Many people believe that kangaroos are threatened by shooting (though none of the species on the verge of extinction is actually hunted).

Note that in this second example the full stop is placed outside the closing bracket, to show that the parenthesis (see below, B5) is only part of the sentence. When the parenthesis forms an independent sentence, the full stop is put inside the final bracket. The position of the full stop after a quotation (see below, B3) is decided in the same way.

2. QUESTION MARK

To show that the preceding sentence forms a direct question, for example:
Who was there?

Note: Indirect questions, that is, ones that form the subordinate or dependent part of a sentence (see chapter 8, pages 103 to 104) are not given question marks:
He asked who was there.

3. EXCLAMATION MARK

To show that the preceding words form an independent exclamation, for example:
What an idea!
As in this example, exclamations often consist of less than the full S + P unit (see page 103). Because they seem to demand an emotional rather than an intellectual response from the reader, exclamation marks are frowned upon in academic writing.

Note: Although exclamation marks are used to emphasize commands in some dramatic kinds of writing, they are not likely to be needed for this purpose in academic writing. Only a very low-key kind of command is likely to be used in an intellectual discussion, for example, *Consider the case of . . . ,* and these need no exclamation mark.

B. For the minor breaks – within sentences

1. SEMICOLON

(a) To separate independent main statements in the same sentence when they are not linked by a conjunctive, for example:
The inquiry began that week; there was a flurry of activity.

Note: These statements could stand equally well as independent sentences:

The inquiry began that week. There was a flurry of activity.
Alternatively, you could use a comma and a conjunctive to link them within the same sentence:
The inquiry began that week, and there was a flurry of activity.

(b) To act as a higher grade of punctuation in setting out a series. Normally this would be done by means of commas (see below, 4(a)). But when commas are also needed for the internal punctuation of one or more items in the series, a different mark is needed for the boundaries between the items, and the semicolon is called in. For example:

The book's readership might include trainee teachers; practising teachers who are now, because of departmental policy, confronted with limited numbers of handicapped children in regular classes; and department planners themselves, who need to be informed about the practical outcomes of their policies.

2. COLON

(a) To show that what follow are either examples of a restatement of what has just been said, thus:

The readers would all be involved with teaching: as trainee teachers, practising teachers, or educational policy makers. (examples)

The book describes his numerous visits to little-known islands of Melanesia: an odyssey in the South Pacific. (restatement)

(b) To precede a quotation of direct speech, for example:
There he declared: "We will bury you."

Note: A comma may be used instead of a colon before a directly quoted speech.

3. QUOTATION MARKS (INVERTED COMMAS)

(a) To show that the words enclosed were the ones actually uttered, as in *"We will bury you"*. On the position of the full stop, see A1.

(b) To emphasize that certain words represent an individual comment or attitude, for example:
His lectures, like his publications, express a "take it or leave it" orientation to his audience.

Note: When two grades of quotation marks are needed, as, for example, when a foreign word turns up in a quotation, single quotation marks are used for the internal punctuation and double quotation marks for the whole quotation, for example:

> *The report says: "There are examples of the 'manana' attitude at all levels of the organization."*

4. COMMA

(a) To separate items in a simple series, for example:

> *The readership is likely to include trainee teachers, practising teachers, and educational policy-makers.*

(b) To set apart a phrase or dependent statement that interrupts the main statement, for example:

> *My cousin, a member of parliament, gave the case some publicity.*
> *My cousin, who felt strongly about it, gave the case some publicity.*

(c) To separate any set of words that would otherwise be misread or altered in meaning, for example:

> *If you want to improve, your approach must be more disciplined.*
> (Without the comma, the sentence is easily misread first time.)
> *They were not optimistic, because they had seen the opinion polls.*
> (Without the comma, the sentence takes on a meaning quite different from the one intended, as if there will be a further explanation of their optimism.)

Note: The presence or absence of a comma can effectively widen or narrow the subject or group under discussion, as in the following:

> *They cannot employ pilots, who are short-sighted.*
> *They cannot employ pilots who are short-sighted.* (Without the comma, the group referred to is smaller and more tightly defined; with the comma, the follow-up comment applies to all of them.)

5. BRACKETS (PARENTHESES)

To show that the words contained are grammatically independent from the sentence around them, for example:

> *She argued in fierce terms (her support for the cause was always vehement), but it was clear that powerful interests were ranged against her.*

No comma is used before the opening bracket, but after it, any punctuation that is needed to indicate the construction of the carrier sentence would be shown. A whole sentence may also stand alone in brackets when the writer wants to show that it is a digression from the main subject or chief topical progression (on which, see chapter 8, pages 109 to 112).

Note: An interposed phrase is often set off with a pair of dashes, for example:
   She argued in fierce — not to say bitter — terms.
But because (single) dashes are used with gay abandon by some people in informal writing, their overtones are casual, and they should be used sparingly in academic writing.

6. ELLIPSIS MARKS (. . .)
To show where part of a statement has been consciously omitted.

REFERENCING
Referencing is the familiar scholarly practice of referring to the works of other writers, where they have supplied you with source material or particular arguments or ideas. This may not be necessary when the same ideas are written about by many authors in the field, but when you are expressing an idea or argument in the words of a particular author you must acknowledge him/her as your source. Failure to do so is a form of plagiarism (passing off someone else's work as your own), and it incurs heavy penalties.

References are at the same time an acknowledgment of your debt to others in the field and a declaration of the body of fact and opinion that backs up your discussion and your conclusions. They are thus a sign of careful scholarship, though there may also be an element of academic showmanship about them. The actual density of references should vary with the type of writing, and it is naturally higher in surveys you make of the relevant literature (including those in the introduction to a report) and lower in writing where you are exploring the logic of your own ideas or reporting your own empirical work.

The first principle of referencing is to make it accurate and unambiguous and to enable the interested reader to check and follow up your sources. But it is also important that references should not distract the reader from the main lines of your discussion. They must be "on call" yet unobtrusive. There are two established methods for achieving this: the footnote/endnote system and the running reference system (also called the Harvard, or author-date system). The first is associated with writing in the humanities, as well as in history and law, while the second is typical of writing in the sciences and history sciences. However, individual departments sometimes have particular policies on referencing, so it is as well to check before writing up an assignment.

Let us consider each system in turn:

1. FOOTNOTE OR ENDNOTE SYSTEMS

This pair of systems keeps reference material out of the ongoing text of the discussion and gathers it together either at the foot of the page (footnotes) or the end of the assignment (endnotes). Within the discussion there are only reference numbers, superscribed above the line at the appropriate point, to refer the reader to a particular reference unit. For endnotes each unit is numbered consecutively through the whole assignment. With footnotes you have the choice of running the numbers consecutively through the whole text or starting afresh with each page. The choice of footnotes or endnotes depends on whether you think your reader needs the references to support his/her reading of the text or just information on where to find them, if necessary. Some writers use footnotes not simply to name a source but to expand on points made in the main discussion. Such notes (known as "substantive footnotes") usually need to be visibly close to the points on which they enlarge.

Whether you opt for footnotes or endnotes, your *first reference* to any work should include full publication details. A first reference to a monograph by a single author would be as follows:

G. Blainey, *Triumph of the Nomads* (Sun Books, Melbourne, 1975), p. 50.

The author's first name may be given in full or just as initials. Publication details nowadays usually include the date of publication, the publishing company and the place of publication; all three are important, since publishing has become a multi-national business. We need to know that a book was published by Edward Arnold in Melbourne, not Edward Arnold in London. It is also helpful to have the publishing company precede the actual place of publication when there are so many publishers in every capital city. This is the practice set forth in the *Australian Government Style Manual*, 3rd ed., though the opposite practice (place before publisher) is adopted in the *Chicago Manual of Style*, 13th ed. (University of Chicago Press, 1982) and its use is certainly not confined to the U.S.A.

When it is a matter of referring to one essay in a published collection by several authors, the details are presented thus:

A. Delbridge, "The recent study of spoken Australian English", in *English Transported*, ed. W. S. Ramson (Australian National University Press, 1970), p. 16.

References to articles that have appeared in journals are much the same:

R. Dabke, "Swearing and abusive language of Australian Rules Football spectators", *Talanya*, vol. 4 (1977), p. 79.

In this, the order of items, the use of inverted commas, the capitalization (proper names only), and the punctuation all conform to common practice, although there are alternatives (see *Chicago Manual of Style*). But whatever practices you adopt, the main thing is to be consistent in your use of them.

Second and later references to the same work are much less detailed: just the minimum needed to distinguish it from any other work cited. If, say, Blainey's *Triumph of the Nomads* (1975) was the only book by that author to which you referred, your later references could be as simple as *Blainey, p. 100*. But if you also referred to, say, Blainey's *Tyranny of Distance* (1966), your later references to either would have to include a date as well, thus *Blainey (1975), p. 100* or *Blainey (1966), p. 100*.

A number of Latin abbreviations are used in some areas of the humanities for second and later references. They include:

ibid. (=in the same place), used when the same work is referred to in two successive notes.

op. cit. (=in the work cited), used to refer to a work on which details have been supplied in an earlier reference, but not the immediately preceding one.

loc. cit. (= in the place cited), used to refer again to the most recently cited passage from the work of a particular author.

Whether you have used endnotes or footnotes, you should also provide at the end of the assignment a bibliography, a complete alphabetical list of the works you have referred to. It may be limited to the works you have actually mentioned in your notes or include others that you looked at but made no specific reference to in the assignment. The latter would be a "List of Works Consulted". The details to be mentioned in a bibliography are almost exactly the same as those of the first reference, and their order and punctuation are the same. One small difference is that the author's surname is put first in each entry so as to set up a clear alphabetic list:

Blainey, G., *Triumph of the Nomads* (Sun Books, Melbourne, 1975).

Blainey, G., *The Tyranny of Distance* (Sun Books, Melbourne, 1966).

If several works by the same author are to be listed, the titles may be in either alphabetical order (as shown here) or chronological order. No particular page references are given for monographs, but with articles in journals or essays from mixed collections the pagination of the whole item is indicated:

Dabke, R., "Swearing and abusive language of Australian Rules Football spectators", *Talanya*, vol. 4 (1977), pp. 76–90.

2. RUNNING REFERENCE SYSTEM
(AUTHOR-DATE, OR HARVARD SYSTEM)

In this system references are included within the main body of the text, enclosed by brackets (parentheses), and kept to the barest minimum. Whether it involves a monograph or a journal article, the first reference gives only the author's surname and the publication date of the work. The following is an example:

. . . In recent accounts of Australian prehistory (Blainey, 1975), more weight has been given to the idea that the Aborigines used fire as a means of managing the land's resources . . .

Page numbers could be added after the date if they were necessary to pinpoint a particular comment, for example (*Blainey*,

1975: 67–83); and the author's initials would be added after his/her surname if there is a possibility of confusion with any other author cited. When there are several co-authors, the surname of each is given in the first reference, but in second and later references the team is referred to by its first member only, followed by *et al.* (=and others). For example, the first reference would appear as: . . . (*Fromkin, Rodman, Collins and Blair, 1983*) . . . , and second and later ones as: . . . (*Fromkin et al., 1983*) . . .

The author–date system relies on a full bibliography at the end to supply the reader with all other details of the publications referred to. Many of the conventions are as for the footnote/endnote bibliography (see page 126), but for the author–date bibliography the titles of works by the same author must be in chronological order, and the date of each work is usually advanced to a position immediately after the author's name:

Blainey, G., 1966. *The Tyranny of Distance* (Sun Books, Melbourne).

Blainey, G., 1975. *Triumph of the Nomads* (Sun Books, Melbourne).

With these points observed, your bibliography will complement the running references fully and efficiently.

APPENDIX A
A few tips on spelling

Every writer's spelling problems are unique. Just which words go wrong depends on all sorts of variables both personal and linguistic, as well as the individual circumstances of writing. Even quite reliable spellers get hung up on certain words occasionally, and few attain dictionary-like perfection all the time.

The fault, if you like, is with the English language, in the many and varied spelling principles it embodies. English has absorbed words from many other languages without modifying their spelling to match its own, and it has hardly modified the spelling of its own words over the last four hundred years in spite of major changes in pronunciation. Many "rules" apply only to small groups of words, and in some cases you just have to know the particular word.

Things are not totally chaotic, however (as is sometimes said), and most student writers manage to spell the short, ordinary words of English quite well, even though those words are among the most irregular of all, for example *any, come, enough, head, heart, women.* The sheer frequency of such words in anything we read drums them in. More problematical are the words that impinge on us less often, the lower-frequency words, usually borrowed from classical languages. They are typically longer and have several syllables, some of which are played down in pronunciation and almost lost. Who could be sure, just from hearing it, that there are three syllables in *ref(e)rence*, and

APPENDIX A

five (or even four) in *contemp((or)a)ry*? On its own, the ear is an unreliable guide to their spelling. But there is help in knowing that *reference* is an extension of *refer*, and that *contemporary* is like *contemporaneous*.

Looking for other related words often helps with the spelling details of longer words. They provide other pegs on which to hang your memory, and they break down the isolation of the problem word. There is no need to get desperate about spelling *despair* (or is it *dispair*?) because both *desperate* and *desperation* can put you right. The different spellings of *persuade* and *pursue* in the first syllable are a nuisance, but you can help yourself by mentally connecting the first with *persuasion* and *persuasive*, and the second with *pursuit*. There are then more words to put you right, and the differences in meaning between the two groups will help to keep them and their spellings apart.

Here is a list of other commonly misspelled words that can be sorted out in the same way:

criticize	NOT critisize	SEE critic, critical
criticism	NOT critisism	SEE critic, critical
definite	NOT definate	SEE finite, definition
grammar	NOT grammer	SEE grammatical, grammarian
integrate	NOT intergrate	SEE integrity, integer
repetition	NOT repitition	SEE repeat, repetitive
satirize	NOT saterize	SEE satire, satirical
sentence	NOT sentance	SEE sententious
separate	NOT seperate	SEE parade, part
substance	NOT substence	SEE substantial, substantive
tendency	NOT tendancy	SEE tendentious
transient	NOT transcient	SEE transition
transience	NOT transcience	SEE transition

This spelling strategy can be applied to many problem words, and it has spin-off for your vocabulary too.

Although most English words are spelled in a standardized way with no deviations allowed, there are a few areas of variability. British and American practice has differed on the ending *-ize/-ise* (as well as *-ization/-isation*) and this leaves you with an option in words like *civilize* and *civilization*. There is, however, a small subset of words that must be spelled with -*ise*, including: *advertise, advise, comprise, compromise, despise, devise, enterprise, excise, exercise, improvise, revise, supervise, surprise, televise*. To get these right you might decide to use -*ise* all the time, and this is the recommendation of *The Macquarie Dictionary* and the *Australian Government Style Manual*. The British/American difference over -*our*/-*or* endings (as in *colour*/*color*) now makes for some interstate differences in Australia. Both spellings are permitted in schools in Victoria and are freely used in Australian newspapers, but the -*our* spelling remains the norm elsewhere.

Britons and Americans also differ over whether to double or not to double the final consonant (especially *l*) in two-syllabled words, before added endings such as -*ed*, -*er* and -*ing*. The British *equalled, kidnapper, signalling* and *traveller* contrast with American *equaled, kidnaper, signaling* and *traveler*, among many examples. (Both, however, agree on doubling when the word has stronger stress on the second syllable, as in *distilled, enrolled*, as long as the syllable has just a one-letter vowel. Neither doubles the consonant in such words as *appealed* or *unveiled*.) But with growing numbers of two-syllabled words like *equal* and *signal* being used as verbs, students here must make a choice between the forms with one *l*, which they encounter in American textbooks, and the double *l* spellings, which are promoted by Australian institutions. The person marking your work may or may not be tolerant of American spelling . . .

One other area of variability is in the spelling of -*ae*- and -*oe*- in words derived through Latin from Greek. The American practice is to reduce them to -*e*-, as in *anemia, feces, fetus, phenix*, while in British/Australian practice they are spelled as *anaemia, faeces, foetus, phoenix*. The vowels -*ae*- and -*oe*- occur in quite a few scientific terms, and you will no doubt be used to seeing them differently spelled, depending on where your reading material was published. In Australia a very few Greek-derived words are now accepted with just -*e*-, for example, *encyclopedia, ether, medieval*, but you would be pioneering with others.

If you use American spellings here you cannot be said to be

wrong, only out of step with the local norms. It is still probably best to wait until you are writing for American journals. In the meantime you may perhaps use a computer spelling check (usually produced in the U.S.A.) and would occasionally find yourself being rapped over the knuckles for *not* using American spellings! Nevertheless, a computer spelling check would help you to pick up many mistakes if you have trouble with the ordinary, high-frequency words of English. It is less help with lower-frequency words and specialized terms.

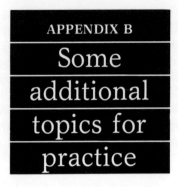

APPENDIX B

Some additional topics for practice

1. Topics in the humanities
(incl. aesthetics, history, linguistics, literature, philosophy)

AESTHETICS
– Discuss the influence on European taste of the discoveries at Pompeii and Herculaneum.
– Discuss changing tastes in landscape gardening in the eighteenth century.

HISTORY
– What was Napoleon's influence on the industrial progress of France?
– Discuss the different views Europeans had of the American Indian in the colonial era.
– Was Captain Cook the greatest navigator of the eighteenth century?
– Wang Mang: callous opportunist or idealistic intellectual?
– What was the nature of the contact between Rome and China during the Han dynasty? Evaluate the evidence attesting to that political contact.
– Compare Achilles and David as embodiments of the heroic ideal of their respective cultures.

LINGUISTICS
– What are the relative merits of the various theories on the origins of language?

– Discuss the concept of arbitrariness in language.
– "Writing is merely a device for recording speech." How well does this account for the relationship between the two media?

LITERATURE
– Discuss the treatment and significance of setting in any modern novel.
– Many modern plays can best be described as "a mirthless howl". Do you agree?
– Compare the treatment of death in the poems of Robert Frost and Robert Lowell.
– What support does *Moll Flanders* give to Daniel Defoe's reputation as the first English novelist?
– What do you consider to be the main themes of Radiguet's *Le Diable au Corps*?
– Compare the use of the first person narrative in Boll's *Uber die Brucke* and Langgaser's *Untergetaucht*.

PHILOSOPHY
– How did Socrates argue that there is a God? Was he right?
– What is ideology? Is there an important distinction between ideology as theory and ideology as practice?
– "I have written some meditations, rather than disputes or questions as the philosophers do . . . in order to testify that I have only written for those who will be willing to seriously meditate with me and consider things with attention . . ." Is Descartes suggesting what philosophy should be?

2. Topics in the sciences
(incl. agriculture, biology, chemistry, engineering, geology, physics, physiology, psychology)

AGRICULTURE
– Discuss the ways in which temperature influences crop growth.
– Discuss the essential features of trickle irrigation and the reasons for its use in certain countries.

BIOLOGY
– Comment on the claim that the Australian flora is adapted to fire.
– Compare the advantages and disadvantages of exoskeletons and endoskeletons.
– What are the principles of the Linnaean system of classification?
– Explain the significance of the seed in the evolution of land plants.

CHEMISTRY
– Give an account of DNA replication.
– Write an essay on hydrogen bonding and the structure of water.

ENGINEERING
– Describe some applications of reinforced earth and the analyses required for the design of reinforced earth structures.
– "The sun does not shine all day." Discuss the problems this causes in solar energy systems and some of the ways of solving these problems.

GEOLOGY
– What factors are involved in the generation of landslides and related phenomena?
– Write an essay on waves in shallow water.
– "The biosphere is involved in all earth processes." Discuss.
– "Mountain glacial landscapes are prime examples of polygenesis and polycyclicity." Discuss.

PHYSICS
– Discuss the standards presently adopted for mass, length and time measurements.
– Describe one application of lasers that makes use of the monochromatic nature of their radiation.
– Outline the major stages of stellar evolution, according to current theories.

PHYSIOLOGY
– Discuss the development of nerve cells within the embryo.
– Discuss the role of biorhythmicity in the physiological control of vertebrate behaviour.
– Describe the structure and function of the larynx.

PSYCHOLOGY
– What does the study of illusions tell us about normal perceptual processes?
– What is control system analysis, and what relevance has it to psychology?

3. Topics in the social sciences
(incl. demography, economics, education (and educational psychology), history, linguistics, politics, sociology)

DEMOGRAPHY
– Write an essay on the nature of urban systems in more and less developed countries.
– Compare the main strengths and weaknesses of medieval and early modern population data.

ECONOMICS
– What determines market structure?
– What are the arguments for and against monopolies?
– Assess the evidence for the proposition that excessive growth of the money supply will cause inflation.
– Outline the various factors that affect the diffusion of new technology in industry.
– What were the main obstacles to capital formation in pre-industrial European society?

EDUCATION AND EDUCATIONAL PSYCHOLOGY
– How does the socialization of a child within a family affect what he/she learns at school?
– In what way does Piaget's view of intelligence differ from the traditional or psychometric approach?
– Discuss the problems in an age-graded education system.

– Outline the salient features of self-concept.
– Describe some of the special problems of the adolescent suffering from a physical handicap.

HISTORY
– Explain why magic, witchcraft and superstition loomed so large in early modern times.
– Why did the Reformation begin in Germany?
– Discuss how the mercantilist policy of the sixteenth and seventeenth centuries affected poverty and vagrancy at that time.
– Why was there such a strong anti-Chinese feeling in Australia during the gold rush period?
– Was Israel the first or last national state in the region?

LINGUISTICS
– Is Australia a multilingual country?
– "The relationship between the development of language and cognitive development is catalytic." Discuss.

POLITICS
– Does the Australian Constitution need to be reformed?
– "The Liberal Party has one principle, and that is to gain office." Discuss.

SOCIOLOGY
– Are there unique roles for mothers and fathers?
– "Women provoke rape by arousing sexual desire and then refusing the consequences." Discuss.
– "Mental illness has more in common with crime than with organic disease, despite the fact that its treatment is in the hands of the medical profession." Discuss.

General index

(and index of writing problems – shown with asterisk)

paragraphing 112–14. *See also* index sentence
parentheses. *See* brackets
passive constructions 73; 107–109
persuasion. *See* writing to influence
plagiarism 123
precision 71; 85–86
problem-solution scheme 34; 37
procedures (in reports). *See* method (reports)
process-based scheme 28
proposition 13; 19–22; 49; 57; 60; 88. *See also* alternative interpretations, evaluation, generalization, interpretation
punctuation 116–23. *See also* colon, comma, etc.
*purpose. *See* proposition, writing to influence

question (to be answered) ch. 2
question mark 120
quotation marks 119; 122
quotations 56–57

*"rambling". *See* purpose, topical progression
*reader. *See* conclusion (essay), interpersonal role of words, introduction (essay), technical terms, values, writing to influence
reasons. *See* argumentation, argumentative writing
referencing 123–27
referential role of words 84–88
*relevance. *See* proposition, selectiveness
report writing (general) 69–70; 81

report format. *See* conclusion (reports), discussion (reports), introduction (reports), method (reports), results
results (presenting experimental results) 76–77; 79

scales
  in exposition 32
  in evaluation 45; 47
schemes for structuring writing ch. 3
scientific method 4–7; 69–70; 73–76; 80
selectiveness 19–20; 40; 43; 72
semicolon 121
sentences
  long 101–102
  simple, compound, complex 102–107
sentence focus. *See* topic and comment
slash mark 119
spelling 128–31
stops (full stops) 119
structure (of physical object) 66–67; 74
structure
  markers in (essay, paper) 55; 57–58; 97–98
  of essay, paper, when writing to influence 37–38; 43–45; 47; 49. *See also* argumentative strategies, body, conclusion (essay), introduction (essay), and table 2 (p. 58)
  of essay, paper, when writing to inform. *See* schemes, and table 2 (p. 58)

First published 1985 by
John Wiley & Sons
65 Park Road, Milton, Qld 4064
140A Victoria Road, Gladesville, N.S.W. 2111
90 Ormond Road, Elwood, Vic. 3184
303 Wright Street, Adelaide, S.A. 5000
4 Kirk Street, Grey Lynn, Auckland 2, N.Z.

Typeset in 10/12 pt Garth

Printed in Hong Kong

© Pam Peters 1985

National Library of Australia
Cataloguing-in-Publication data

Peters, Pam.
  Strategies for student writers.

  Includes index.
  ISBN 0 471 33406 5.

  1. English language – Rhetoric. 2. English
  language – Style. I. Title.

808'.042

effectiveness on ha
onventional, as w
ers supply the sta
chapter
cture. Y
s the sha
matter

Strategies
for student
writers

**A guide to writing essays,
tutorial papers,
exam papers and reports**

Pam Peters

John Wiley & Sons

**Brisbane   New York
Chichester   Toronto**

nd ideall
haracter
message
betweer
e best order or arr;
res the organizing
structures are illus
assignment topics